Men-at-Arms • 445

Medieval Polish Armies 966–1500

W Sarnecki & D Nicolle · Illustrated by Gerry Embleton

Series editor Martin Windrow

First published in Great Britain in 2008 by Osprey Publishing,
Midland House, West Way, Botley, Oxford OX2 0PH, UK
443 Park Avenue South, New York, NY 10016, USA

E-mail: **info@ospreypublishing.com**

© 2008 Osprey Publishing Ltd.

A CIP catalogue record for this book is available from the British Library

ISBN: 978 1 84603 014 7

Edited by Martin Windrow
Page layout by Alan Hamp
Index by Glyn Sutcliffe
Typeset in Helvetica Neue and ITC New Baskerville
Originated by PPS Grasmere Ltd
Printed in China through Worldprint

08 09 10 11 12   10 9 8 7 6 5 4 3 2 1

FOR A CATALOGUE OF ALL BOOKS PUBLISHED BY
OSPREY MILITARY AND AVIATION PLEASE CONTACT:

North America
Osprey Direct, c/o Random House Distribution Center, 400 Hahn Road,
Westminster, MD 21157 USA
E-mail: info@ospreydirect.com

All other regions
Osprey Direct UK, P.O. Box 140 Wellingborough, Northants, NN8 2FA, UK
E-mail: info@ospreydirect.co.uk

Osprey Publishing is supporting the Woodland Trust, the UK's leading
woodland conservation charity, by funding the dedication of trees.

www.ospreypublishing.com

Artist's note

Readers may care to note that the original paintings from which the
colour plates in this book were prepared are available for private
sale. All reproduction copyright whatsoever is retained by the
Publishers. All enquiries should be addressed to:

www.gerryembleton.com

The Publishers regret that they can enter into no correspondence
upon this matter.

MEDIEVAL POLISH ARMIES
c.960–1525

HISTORICAL BACKGROUND

POLAND BECAME A Christian country in AD 966, and in military terms the state was unified under the rule of Prince Mieszko I. However, the new kingdom was constantly threatened by numerous enemies, and consequently Mieszko and his successors were obliged to recognize the Western or German Emperors – later known as the Holy Roman Emperors – as their overlords. At the same time they often continued to find themselves in conflict with neighbouring German feudal lords, as well as with the Emperors themselves. Other foes during these early centuries included the pagan tribes of Pomerania; the Russians, including those now identified as Belarussians and Ukrainians; and the Bohemians (Czechs). Such conflicts were partly in defence of the newly formed Kingdom of Poland, and partly wars of conquest or expansion by the Poles themselves. In military terms this period was typified by units of professional household troops called the *druzhina*, who were supported during wartime by local militias or *woye*.

The next period of Polish history is known as the Division in the Provinces, and lasted from 1138 to 1320. This long era of fragmentation was characterized by a decline of part-time militias in favour of professional – or at least, better-trained – household and local troops. It was upon these that the rulers of Poland now relied. It was also during this period, from the mid-12th to early 14th century, that a true Polish knightly class emerged as part of a gradually developing feudal system of government and social organization. Furthermore, in 1154–55 the crusading military orders – the Hospitallers and Templars – gained their first footholds on Polish soil. Later in this notably turbulent period the Teutonic Knights joined the older-established military orders, arriving on the scene in 1226, almost simultaneously with the foundation of the specifically Polish Brethren of Dobrzyn (Knights of Christ). Then came the Mongol invasions, with raids deep into Europe that culminated in the battle of Liegnitz/Legnica in 1241.

Detail from 'David and Goliath' on an embossed chalice, dating from c.1175–1200. Note the sword passing through a slit in the left hip of the mail hauberk, and the kite-shaped shield. (Abbey of Tzemeszno)

3

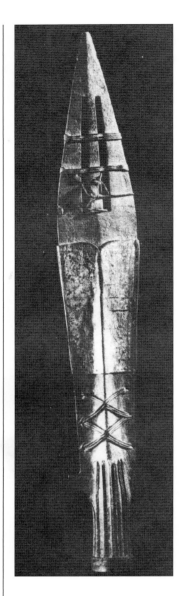

The so-called 'Spear of St Maurice' was given to Boleslaw I of Poland by Emperor Otto III of Germany in AD 1000. It is a simplified version of the so-called 'Holy Imperial Spear' of the Western Empire. (Cathedral Treasury, Wawel, Cracow)

The 14th century saw the reunification of Poland under the rule of King Wladyslaw I Lokietek, known as 'the Short', and his son Casimir III, 'the Great'. It also witnessed a growing threat from the Teutonic Knights, until the latter were defeated at the battle of Plowce in 1331. As a consequence of his relatively peaceful reign, King Casimir III went down in Polish history as one of the country's greatest administrators and castle-builders; about 80 strongholds were constructed during his time.

In 1370 the still relatively small Kingdom of Poland was joined with the sprawling Angevin state in Central Europe, based upon the Kingdom of Hungary. This was, however, merely a personal union, that came about when King Louis of Hungary succeeded the childless Casimir the Great as ruler of Poland; it fell apart soon after Louis' own death, there being little or no economic, political, ethnic or even strategic reason for its continuing existence.

The Jagiello dynasty and union with Lithuania
There now followed one of the most significant events in medieval European history, when one of King Louis' daughters, Jadwiga, was betrothed to the pagan Lithuanian Grand Duke Jogaila in 1386. Jogaila was baptized as a Christian, and his already huge Lithuanian state similarly became at least officially Christian in the process, Jogaila himself ruling as King Wladyslaw II Jagiello of Poland and Lithuania.

The history of later medieval Poland cannot be properly understood without looking at the history of its neighbour, rival and now partner Lithuania. This is equally true of later medieval Polish armies; these would develop to a large extent along highly distinctive lines, which set them apart from the military forces of Poland's western and Baltic neighbours. The Mongol invasion and conquest of most of the Russian principalities in the 13th century, and their domination by the Mongol Golden Horde successor state, shattered the previous political and military order. This in turn enabled the small, largely pagan and in many respects still tribal Grand Duchy of Lithuania to expand at the expense of its Russian neighbours to the south-east, taking over several Russian principalities starting with Polotsk. This remarkable and still theoretically pagan expansion continued throughout the 14th century, eventually overrunning the whole of southern or Kievan Russia up to the frontier with the now declining Mongol Golden Horde. The once powerful Mongols were themselves pushed back in their turn, and by 1392 the Lithuanians had reached the north-western shores of the Black Sea. By that date, of course, the now vast Grand Duchy of Lithuania was a Christian state, and was six years into its union with emphatically Catholic Christian Poland. Nevertheless, the two 'united' states continued to operate and function separately, only really joining forces to fight common foes such as the Teutonic Knights.

The 15th century was a period of significant change for medieval Polish armies, as it was for armies across most of Europe. The Teutonic Knights suffered a further and even more catastrophic defeat in 1410 at the battle of Tannenberg/Grunwald, where they were defeated by King Wladyslaw II Jagiello of Poland-Lithuania. The following year the Peace of Thorn/Torun ended what is known as 'The Great War against the Teutonic Order'. Jagiello's son, Wladislaw III Warnenczyk, the young king of both Poland-Lithuania and Hungary, now focused the country's military efforts to the east and south in an effort to combat Ottoman Turkish expansion; however, he was killed at the battle of Varna in 1444.

Wladislaw III's brother and successor, Casimir IV Jagiellonczyk, looked north again in an effort to retain Pomerania. He decided to support a revolt in Prussia against the rule of the Teutonic Knights, thus beginning what is known as 'The Thirteen Years' War'. It was this conflict that saw the large-scale introduction of mercenary troops into Polish armies, along with Hussite *wagenburg* tactics, more advanced siege methods, and naval warfare. The latter was a relatively new phenomenon for Poland, which had previously been a usually land-locked state. Siege and naval warfare dominated the later stages of the war with the Teutonic Knights, which was finally won in 1466 as a result of sophisticated combined land and naval operations by Polish troops.

Effigial brass of Lukasz of Górka, the *voivode* or governor of Poznan, made around 1488. His sallet helmet and full 'Gothic' armour are entirely within the Western European tradition of the late 15th century. (*in situ* Cathedral, Poznan)

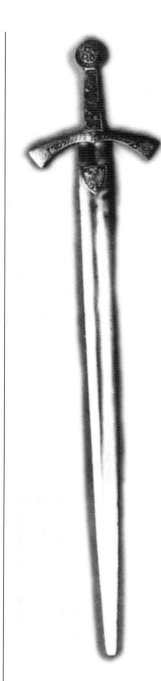

The Polish kingdom's coronation sword, known as *Szczerbiec*. The blade supposedly belonged to the first Polish ruler, Boleslaw 'the Brave', but the earliest confirmed reference to it is during the coronation of Wladyslaw I in 1320. (Wawel Castle, Cracow)

The 16th century

The reign of Jan I Olbracht, with his disastrous Moldavian campaign of 1497 against the Ottoman Turks, effectively ended the medieval period in Polish military history. However, the power of the Jagiello dynasty grew and for some time seemed to flourish, though in reality its foundations were archaic and weakening. The long-established Jagiello dynastic connection with Hungary resulted in another 'personal union' between Hungary and Bohemia under Jagiello rulers, which lasted from 1490 until 1526. As before, however, the constituent parts remained separate kingdoms with almost entirely separate military and administrative structures. In 1506 the governor of Silesia became King of Poland and Grand Duke of Lithuania as Sigismund I 'the Old', while the originally Lithuanian Jagiello dynasty continued to rule Hungary and Bohemia until 1526. Jagiello rule would also continue in Poland-Lithuania beyond the middle of the 16th century, and would be followed by another form of union or 'commonwealth'. This in turn endured until the partition of Poland by her stronger neighbours in the late 18th century, after which the country disappeared as an independent entity – apart from the brief period of the Duchy of Warsaw under Napoleonic domination – until 1918.

CHRONOLOGY

10th century:
c.960–992 Reign of Mieszko I
963–964 First raids of German Count Wichmann reach territory of Mieszko I
966 Mieszko I accepts Christianity – the 'Baptism of Poland'
979 Invasion by Emperor Otto II ends with a peace treaty; Mieszko becomes an Imperial ally
992–1025 Reign of Boleslaw I 'the Brave'

11th century:
1000 Congress of Gniezno – meeting between Boleslaw and the German Emperor Otto III, who recognizes Boleslaw as sovereign ruler of Poland and presents him with 'The Spear of St Maurice'
1003–18 Wars between Poland and the German King Henry II
1003 Boleslaw enters Prague and is acclaimed ruler of Bohemia
1005 Poland cedes Lusatia and Milsko to Germany
1007 Poland regains Lusatia and Milsko
1013 Peace of Merseburg: Poland holds Lusatia and Milsko as a fief under the Emperor.
1018 Polish war against Russia; Boleslaw invades the Principality of Kiev and defeats Jaroslaw the Wise at the battle of the River Bug
1025–34 Reign of Mieszko II Lambert
1029–31 Polish war against German Emperor Conrad II
1031 Mieszko II trapped by simultaneous German and Russian invasions; cedes Milsko and Lusatia to the Emperor
1034–58 Reign of Casimir I 'the Restorer'
1034 Peasants' revolt and pagan reaction; Casimir I flees the country
1039–41 Casimir I, supported by Emperor Henry III, returns to Poland
1050 Casimir I recaptures Silesia

1058–79 Reign of Boleslaw II 'the Bold'
1069 Boleslaw II invades the Principality of Kiev
1077 Second Polish invasion of Kiev
1079 Boleslaw II forced to flee the country
1079–1102 Reign of Wladyslaw I Herman

12th century:
1102–38 Reign of Boleslaw III 'Wry-mouth'
1102–24 Struggle for control of Pomerania
1109 German-Bohemian invasion of Poland
1110 Boleslaw III invades Bohemia
1113–22 Polish reconquest of Eastern and Western Pomerania
1138 Death of Boleslaw III, leaving Poland divided among his numerous sons, with one recognized as senior *princeps*
1138–1320 Period of 'Division in the Provinces':
1157 Foundation of the German Margravate of Brandenburg; invasion of Poland by German Emperor Frederick I Barbarossa; Duke Boleslaw IV 'the Curly' pays homage to the Emperor

13th century:
1205 Invading army of ruler of the Russian principality of Galich-Vladimir defeated at Zawichost
1227 Assassination of the last *princeps*, Duke Leszek 'the White' of Cracow, removes last vestiges of central power
1226–30 The Teutonic Order arrives in Prussia
1228 Foundation of the Polish crusading military order of the Brethren of Dobrzyn

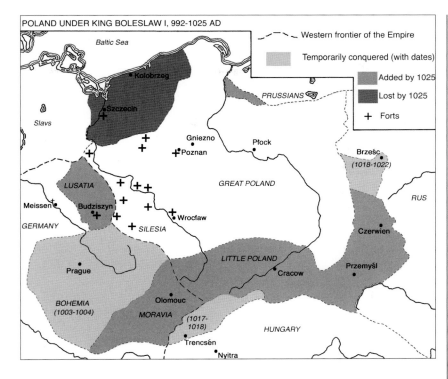

POLAND UNDER KING BOLESLAW I, 992-1025 AD

- - - Western frontier of the Empire
▨ Temporarily conquered (with dates)
▨ Added by 1025
■ Lost by 1025
+ Forts

Baltic Sea
• Kolobrzeg
PRUSSIANS
Szczecin ✚
Slavs
Gniezno •
Płock •
✚Poznan
Brześc (1018-1022)
GREAT POLAND
RUS
LUSATIA
Meissen•
Budziszyn •
Wrocław
GERMANY
SILESIA
Czerwien •
LITTLE POLAND
Przemyśl •
Prague •
Cracow •
BOHEMIA (1003-1004)
Olomouc •
MORAVIA
(1017-1018)
HUNGARY
Trencsén •
• Nyitra

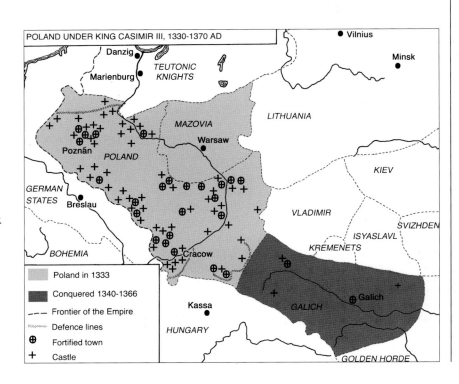

POLAND UNDER KING CASIMIR III, 1330-1370 AD

• Vilnius
Danzig •
Minsk •
TEUTONIC KNIGHTS
Marienburg •
LITHUANIA
MAZOVIA
Poznań •
Warsaw •
POLAND
KIEV
GERMAN STATES
Breslau •
VLADIMIR
SVIZHDEN
BOHEMIA
ISYASLAVL
KREMENETS
Cracow •
Galich ⊕
Kassa •
GALICH
HUNGARY
GOLDEN HORDE

▨ Poland in 1333
■ Conquered 1340-1366
- - - Frontier of the Empire
〰 Defence lines
⊕ Fortified town
+ Castle

7

1235 The Teutonic Knights, supported by
Polish and Pomeranian crusaders, crush the
pagan Prussians; the Brethren of Dobrzyn
are incorporated into the Teutonic Order

1241 First Mongol invasion of Poland; Duke
Henry II 'the Pious' is killed at the battle
of Liegnitz

1259–60 Second Mongol invasion of Poland

1287–88 Third Mongol invasion repulsed by
Polish and Hungarian troops

1295–96 Reign of Premislas II, Duke of Poznan,
as King of Poland

14th century:

1300–05 Reign of Wenceslaus II, King of
Bohemia, under whose rule most Polish
territory is reunified

1306–33 Reign of Wladyslaw I 'the Elbow-High'

1326–29 War between Poland and Margravate
of Brandenburg

1327–32 War between Poland and the Teutonic
Order

1333–70 Reign of Casimir III 'the Great'

1340–66 Polish conquest of Russian Principality
of Galich

1345–48 Struggle for control of Silesia

1370–82 Reign of Louis I 'the Great' of Hungary, who designates
his mother Elisabeth – the sister of Casimir the Great – as regent
in Poland

1382–84 Interregnum
after the death of Louis
I, followed by civil war

1384 Jadwiga of Anjou,
daughter of Louis I, is
crowned 'king' of
Poland

1385–87 Grand Duke
Jogaila of Lithuania
accepts Christianity
in return for Polish
throne; he marries
Jadwiga, and rules
as King Wladyslaw II
Jagiello from 1386
to 1434

15th century:

1401–02 Teutonic Knights
raid now-Christian
Lithuania

1409–11 'Great War'
between Poland-

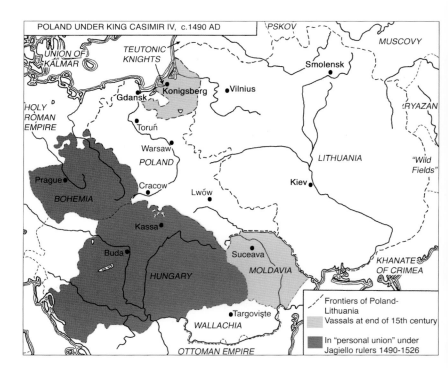

POLAND UNDER KING CASIMIR IV, c.1490 AD

PSKOV
MUSCOVY
UNION OF KALMAR
TEUTONIC KNIGHTS
Smolensk
Konigsberg
Gdansk
Vilnius
HOLY ROMAN EMPIRE
RYAZAN
Toruń
Warsaw
POLAND
LITHUANIA
"Wild Fields"
Prague
BOHEMIA
Cracow
Lwów
Kiev
Kassa
Buda
Suceava
KHANATE OF CRIMEA
HUNGARY
MOLDAVIA
Targovişte
WALLACHIA
OTTOMAN EMPIRE

- - - Frontiers of Poland-Lithuania
Vassals at end of 15th century
In "personal union" under Jagiello rulers 1490-1526

OPPOSITE The castle of Bedzin, which was constructed by King Casimir the Great around 1349. The map on page 7 shows the remarkable increase in Polish fortified places during this monarch's long reign.

Lithuania and Teutonic Order; Teutonic Knights defeated at battle of Tannenberg

1411 War ends with Treaty of Torun/Thorn

1419 War between Teutonic Order–Brandenburg alliance and alliance of Poland with King Eric VII of Sweden, Denmark and Norway

1420–22 Bohemian Hussite sect offers crown of Bohemia to King Wladyslaw Jagiello; this is accepted by Grand Duke Vytautas of Lithuania, whose nephew Sigismund Korybutas becomes Polish-Lithuanian governor in Bohemia

1428–33 Hussite movement spreads in Silesia

1432 Poland forms alliance with Hussites against Teutonic Order

1434–44 Reign of Vladislaus III (as king of both Poland and Hungary from 1440)

1439 Polish Hussites are defeated by royal troops at battle of Grotniki

1441–43 Hungarian–Ottoman war, concluding with Peace of Szeged

1444 Vladislaus III breaks the truce and invades Ottoman territory, and is killed when his multinational Crusader army is crushed at Varna

1444–47 Interregnum in Poland

1447–92 Reign of Casimir IV Jagiellon, brother of Vladislaus III, who had ruled as Grand Duke of Lithuania since 1440

1454–66 'Thirteen Years' War' between Poland and Teutonic Order

1463 Battle of the Vistula Lagoon: Teutonic Knights' fleet defeated by ships from Danzig and Elbing

1466 Second Treaty of Thorn/Torun; Teutonic Order becomes a vassal of the Polish Crown

1475–76 Ottoman Turks raid Moldavia but are defeated by the Moldavian *voivode* Stefan 'the Great', currently a vassal of Poland

1487–91 Crimean Tartars raid eastern territories of Poland-Lithuania as allies of the Ottoman sultan

1492–1501 Reign of John I Albert

1492–94 War between Muscovy and Lithuania, ending with marriage of Alexander Jagiellon, Grand Duke of Lithuania, to Tsar Ivan III's daughter Helen

1498 First Ottoman incursions into Poland

16th century:

1501–06 Reign of Alexander I Jagiellon

1506–48 Reign of Sigismund I 'the Old', former governor of Silesia, as King of Poland and Grand Duke of Lithuania

1514 Muscovite army defeated by Polish-Lithuanian force at battle of Orsha

1519–21 Last war between Poland and Teutonic Order

1525 'The Homage of Prussia': Teutonic Grand Master Albrecht Hohenzollern-Ansbach swears allegiance to King Sigismund I; secularization of the Teutonic Order

ORGANIZATION OF POLISH ARMIES

When Poland accepted Christianity in AD 966 the country was, in military terms, unified under the rule of Prince Mieszko I. Mieszko is also regarded as the first truly historical figure in the history of the Polish state; but the

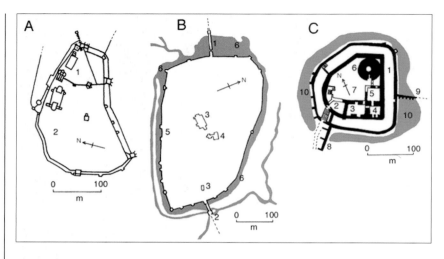

new kingdom already had its government, administration and military system established by that time, these apparently having emerged at an earlier but unrecorded date. This first system of military administration was based upon a series of strongholds, each of which was governed by a *castellan*. Groups of neighbouring *castellanies* formed a province, which was in turn ruled by a powerful individual known in Latin as a *comes provinti* or in Slavic early Polish as a *voivode*.

Polish fortifications, 11th–14th centuries (after Kaufmann & Kaufmann):
(A) *Wawel of Krakow*: (1) upper castle, (2) lower castle.
(B) *Osno*: (1 & 2) bridged gates, (3) town hall, (4) churches, (5) postern, (6) wet moat.
(C) *Bedzin Castle:* (1) outer bailey, (2) main gate, (3) great hall, (4) square tower, (5) administrative building, (6) keep, (7) inner bailey, (8) foregate, (9) curtain wall, (10) dry moat.

BELOW **(Left)** A mid-14th-century bascinet with an attachment point for a removable visor; found at Sandomierz. It is thought to have been fitted with a folding crown, and thus to have belonged to King Casimir the Great. **(Right)** A helmet found near Torun, whose unusual shape recalls examples from 13th-century nomad graves in the Ukraine. (Local Museum, Torun)

The rulers of Poland's first dynasty, the Piast kings, would travel around the country accompanied by their retinues, since they did not have their own permanent abode or capital. This was, of course, a system that had been known across most of Europe during the early Middle Ages and was still common in many countries. In Poland, as elsewhere, this 'rule from the saddle' made it easier for monarchs to control their local or provincial representatives, to judge the loyalty of their liege-men, and to collect taxes. This system was known in the early Polish state as 'prince's law'; its effectiveness was frequently tested by various external and internal challenges, and it reached its zenith during the reign of Boleslaw I Chrobry 'the Brave' (992–1025).

Household troops

The system of household troops or *druzhina* had its origins in the undocumented period prior to the emergence and rise of the first Piast ruling dynasty, when groups of warriors served as a tribal chieftain's personal guard. Such military followings had gradually become more dependent upon, and loyal to, their chieftain rather than to their tribe as a whole. Partially as a result of this increasingly reliable military resource, a chieftain's right to rule gradually became both unquestioned and hereditary.

The first written evidence for such Polish and other north-western Slav tribal *druzhinas* is found in the account by the Andalusian Jewish slave-trader Abraham Ben Yacob of his journey across the Slavonic countries in the second half of the 10th century. Abraham describes these forces as consisting of professional warriors who were armed and maintained, along with their families, by their prince. Their status as heavy cavalrymen was clearly defined by the use of the Latin term *loricati* or 'armoured ones'.

Each *druzhina* was supposedly divided into at least two groups, the most important of which were the prince's truly élite but also considerably less numerous bodyguards, who would later be known as the *acies curialis*. They were almost full-time soldiers at the ruler's immediate disposal, and as such they took part in virtually all military operations, especially during offensive campaigns. It was also from their ranks that the prince drew his most trusted friends and advisers, and consequently this relatively small corps of bodyguards also took the lion's share of any spoils. The remaining members of the *druzhina* were used to garrison smaller outposts, sometimes far from the main centres of population, where they also controlled the inhabitants and collected local taxes. They are also believed to have supervised the so-called 'serviceable settlements', especially those whose primary purpose was to work for and to support the army.

The levy

In addition to his *druzhina* the prince could rely on the levy of all free men eligible for military service. This was a considerably larger group of potential combatants, whose origin could be traced back to the early tribal tradition of the so-called primary levy-en-masse. Its recruitment base had by now increased; in addition to the peasants and serfs, there were also the numerous inhabitants of the more recently established strongholds, as well as the *milites* or individual warriors who did not form part of a *druzhina* but could be mobilized in case of war. The great majority of these fighting men were infantry, and were expected to arm themselves at their own expense. They were also defined as *clipeati* or shield-bearers, this being their main (and in many cases, their only) form of protection.

Despite an effectiveness that was proved in several conflicts, this levy-en-masse was soon found to be inadequate. One of its main weaknesses seems to have been, paradoxically, its very size: the levy often appeared in large numbers that were difficult to control during a campaign. Its members were also, of course, much less disciplined than the *druzhina*, and as a result the role of the originally tribal levy was soon limited to the defence of a territory under direct attack or invasion. Equally significantly, the rural serfs were needed to fulfill other tasks, such as the *custodia* – maintaining guard over a local outpost. On the other hand the levy of low-status personnel continued to prove useful for harassing or pursuing a broken enemy.

The decline of the *druzhina*

Another major military change occurred during the second half of the 11th century. During this period the prince's personal following or *druzhina* began to lose its pre-eminent position, in favour of the lords

Effigy of Duke Bolko II of Ziebice and his wife, Jutta, c.1342; note the shield blazon – compare this with the picture on page 43. (*in situ* Cistercian Abbey, Henvyków)

or higher aristocracy; these were increasingly capable of fielding their own household troops, even though these forces were each less numerous that the ruler's *druzhina*. It was at around this same time that the number of heavy or fully armoured cavalrymen increased within Polish armed forces, and the earlier levy-en-masse evolved into a more limited, but better equipped, levy of knights.

Theoretically at least, these early Polish forces were organized on the basis of threes and tens, and were supposedly divided into territorial units. In reality, however, their true numbers are very difficult to reconstruct; though Poland was said to have been able to field some 200,000 men in the 10th and 11th centuries, the actual numbers were almost certainly much smaller.

The next period of Polish history was that of the so-called Division in the Provinces, which began with the death of Boleslaw III Krzywousty 'Wry-mouth' in 1138. Conscious of the danger of civil war, this ruler divided his domains among his numerous sons but designated one of them as his successor, to be superior to his brothers. Unfortunately but predictably, Boleslaw's plan failed; the country soon fragmented into a number of competing duchies, whose rulers sought political advantage over their rivals and frequently fought one another. Meanwhile, since the senior nobility often held domains that were scattered all over the country, this inevitably drew them into the complex power struggles that came to characterize Polish history during these turbulent two centuries.

Another very important but potentially problematic feature of later 12th- and early 13th-century Poland was the increasing colonization of many parts of the country by German settlers, both urban and rural, as well as the spreading influence of German law. This Germanization and urbanization had, in fact, started at the turn of 12th century, and consequently many new towns had been founded and fortified. Along with those urban centres that already existed, these new towns considerably increased Poland's military potential. Meanwhile the manufacture of arms, armour, horse-harness and other gear required by Poland's armies was steadily moving away from the old system of 'serviceable settlements', to be replaced by highly specialized urban craft industries.

Economic factors were also among the several reasons for the decline of the prince's *druzhina* during this period, and the last vestiges of those once-formidable warriors were now found in the household military units of dukes and other senior feudal lords. After the effective disbandment of the monarch's *druzhina* the traditional concept of military service in return for maintenance or money payment was replaced by service as a form of feudal obligation under the *ius militareor* or 'law of knights'. Members of the knightly class, which had

Wierzbięta of Branice, shown as a donor figure on the panel painting of the Virgin Mary and Jesus which he paid for in c.1425.

emerged as a result of these important social and economic changes, were now obliged to offer military service in return for receiving land in the form of fiefs. This was, of course, essentially the same as the feudal system that theoretically underpinned social and military organization in the rest of later medieval Central and Western Europe.

Knight service

These Polish knights, like their German and other neighbours, were expected to arm themselves and their retainers, the numbers of the latter depending upon a knight's wealth and the value of his territorial fief. The most numerous military followings were those of the so-called *barones* or barons, while the *nobiles* or middle-ranking knights led smaller forces; the retinues themselves were made up of warriors who did not usually own land. Alongside these landless fighting men were the 'created knights', maintained or organized by the *advocati* or mayors of Poland's increasing number of towns, and the *sculteti*, who were effectively village administrators or headmen.

The ruler had the right to call upon these knights at any time he considered it necessary, and would employ two distinct forms of mobilization. The first system of service was known as *infra terram*, which meant a summons in defence of the realm. The second was called *extra terram*, which, as its name indicates, meant campaigning outside the country; unlike service *infra terram*, this would be partially reimbursed by the individual warrior's overlord. Unsurprisingly, the first form of summons was considered the more important, and failure to attend could lead to a knight suffering a substantial fine or even having his property and land confiscated.

Serfs and townsmen

While the ruler's *druzhina* declined, the military duties of the serfs were also reduced, with many villages obtaining complete immunities. Those serfs who were still eligible for military service continued to be expected to arm themselves and to take part in campaigns at their own expense. In addition to such duties they were also obliged to repair and maintain the fortifications within their own region. In common with more senior members of society, those serfs who failed in such feudal obligations might also be fined.

At the beginning of the 13th century another group of men who emerged as militarily significant were the inhabitants of the fortified towns that were another new feature of the Polish countryside from this period. While their active duties were largely limited to the defence of their own communities, the urban population were also expected to provide the army with craftsmen and some means of transport, most notably horse-drawn wagons, and sometimes to form a protective escort for such convoys.

Detail from the contemporary effigial slab of Wierzbiêta of Branice. (both *in situ* parish church, Ruszcza)

According to the primary documentary sources, however, the Polish army continued to be mustered as a levy-en-masse, and to be organized around three main groups of combatants. These were the knights, who formed an army's cavalry; the serfs and townsfolk, who fought as infantry, manned the siege weapons and guarded the baggage train; and those troops allocated to garrison various outposts or fortifications.

Unit organization

Very little is known about the structure of smaller military units during this period. Nevertheless, it does appear that the old, traditional decimal system was replaced by one based upon territorial or family units – thus reflecting in some ways the fragmented political situation of the country as a whole. The largest cavalry units seem to have been grouped around and identified by a territorial or family *banner*, the formation itself being made up of a number of smaller units known as *lances*. This was much the same as was seen in Germany or France, with the *lance* – the smallest element in the army's structure – actually consisting of a knight and his retainers, who more often than not were mounted crossbowmen. Individual banners may have differed in size, the number of combatants grouped beneath the flag reflecting the wealth of the lords who led such formations. Other banners may have identified larger territorial or provincial formations consisting of all the forces mustered by a number of lords in that part of the country. The infantry was probably similarly divided into smaller territorial or family units, in accordance with this new system of mustering. The overall commander in each province was the local duke, who would appoint a *voivode* as his second-in-command or as a substitute during his absence.

In broader terms, the military potential of Poland during the period of the Middle Ages remains a matter of scholarly debate and widespread disagreement. According to some demographic researchers, there were theoretically about 23,000 to 25,000 troops available to the Polish provinces if all were mustered at once, which practically never happened. The number necessary for defence of individual Polish outposts probably varied from around 130 to 260 fighting men, depending on the size of the fortification.

* * *

The 14th century saw the reunification of Poland under the rule of King Wladyslaw I Lokietek 'the Short', who came to the throne in 1320. He was faced with numerous opponents and experienced the ups and downs typical of all medieval power struggles; but the main challenge to the Polish monarchy remained that posed by the Teutonic Order in Prussia and Livonia. This religio-military order, though defeated at the battle of Plowce in 1331, continued to be a significant military power that the Polish kings could not ignore. Consequently, the main aim of Wladyslaw I Lokietek's son and successor Casimir III 'the Great' was to further consolidate the military and economic strength of the kingdom

Jan of Ujazd portrayed as a donor figure at prayer before the Virgin Mary and Christchild, on a panel painting made in around 1450. Note the very deep fauld of his armour; and the 'reversed S' shield blazon at top left, typical of a kind of Central European motif quite distinct from the heraldic traditions of the West.

OPPOSITE **Magnificent brass effigial monument, made in c.1475, to Jan Koniecpolski, the Great Chancellor of Poland, and his sons. All three images show classic late 15th-century full-plate armours, over mail at the neck and dagged mail below the faulds; some aspects appear distinctive, and are discussed in the commentary to Plate G1. Note also the blazon of a small cross and a horseshoe on the shields at the knights' feet. (***in situ*** parish church, Wielgomtyny)**

that Wladyslaw had effectively rebuilt. It is worth noting that, despite Casimir the Great's brilliant campaigns – including the conquest of Galich Vladimir in 1340–66 – he is primarily remembered in Polish history as one of the country's greatest administrators and fortifiers, and a remarkable number of castles and other strongpoints were constructed during his reign.

The 15th century was a time of profound change for Polish armed forces. The Teutonic Knights suffered a catastrophic disaster at the battle of Tannenberg/Grunwald in 1410, when they were defeated by King Wladyslaw II Jagiello of Poland-Lithuania; yet even this success did not solve the political problems between Poland and the Order, and hostilities grumbled on for another century or more.

Jagiello's son Wladyslaw III Warnenczyk ruled as king of both Poland and Hungary, putting a great deal of effort into his attempts to halt Ottoman Turkish expansion in the Balkans and south-eastern Europe. However, following a largely successful campaign in 1443 he was defeated and killed at the battle of Varna the following year. His brother and successor, Casimir IV Jagiellonczyk found his efforts diverted northwards to the Baltic coastal regions, where he attempted to regain control of Pomerania. This led Casimir IV to support the revolt against the rule of the Teutonic Knights in Prussia, which resulted in the outbreak of what came to be known as the 'Thirteen Years' War' in 1454. This was waged with varying degrees of success, but eventually ended in Polish military and political victory over the Teutonic Knights in 1466.

Although the reign of Jan I Olbracht in the final decade of the 15th century is widely regarded as the closing chapter in medieval Polish military history, it was also characterized by the increasingly bitter struggle against the expanding

Ottoman Turkish sultanate and empire which would consume so much of Poland's military energy over the coming generations. During the later Middle Ages, however, it was the reunification of Poland which seems to have been the key factor in the reorganization and modernization of her armies. The most significant reforms to the military system were put into effect in accordance with statutes or laws promulgated by King Casimir the Great.

The Casimirian reforms

The forms of service laid down by the king consisted of the *expeditio generalis* or levy of knights; the so-called 'mobilization of domains and towns'; and the *defensio terrae*, or defence of the nation.

An *expeditio generalis* was made up of the aristocracy reinforced with the 'created knights', the latter now including not only *sculteti* village administrators but even some men of serf status. Another group of combatants consisted of the men-at-arms fielded by the clergy and other ecclesistical authorites as their military substitutes. The knights, whose service was still regulated by the *ius militareor* or 'law of the knights', were required to arm themselves and their retinues at their own expense. For service outside the country, these knights could expect to be partially paid by the king, who was also supposed to reimburse them for any losses of equipment or horses. According to 'The Privilege of Koshice' in 1374, Polish knights had the right to be ransomed by their king if they were taken prisoner.

As already stated, the basic cavalry unit was the lance, which usually consisted of three men – the fully armoured knight himself, plus two more lightly equipped retainers. However, this was not a fixed rule; there were many Polish lances made up of one knight plus crossbowmen, while others consisted only of knights or only of crossbowmen.

The most common proportion of heavy to light horsemen seems to have been one to three, with the latter including men who might better be termed mounted infantry. The larger tactical units which existed within the *expeditio generalis* continued to be the 'banners', and these might be structured along territorial or non-territorial lines. In addition to 'district' and 'royal' banners, there were also units assembled and led by leading members of the aristocracy, as well as 'banners' consisting of hired mercenaries. A 'royal banner' called the *Goncza* traditionally served as the vanguard of the army, while another called the *Nadworna* formed the monarch's bodyguard, the latter consisting almost entirely of

A detail from a panel painting of the 'Massacre of the Innocents', made at the close of the 15th century. It illustrates an almost unarmoured light cavalryman (centre) riding beside a man-at-arms in full plate harness (right) – see commentaries to Plate G. The costumes of the peasant reapers (left) are also interesting. (National Museum, Warsaw)

courtiers. Because their domains were scattered all over the kingdom, the knights had the right to choose the unit in which they wished to serve, the only significant exception being the 'Great Cracow Banner', which traditionally consisted of the cream of Polish chivalry.

During the period under consideration the infantry of the Polish kingdom was mainly composed of soldiers who were mustered under the 'mobilization of domains and towns', plus serfs obliged to serve in *defensio terrae*. Another important group of combatants were the urban militias, whose main task was the defence of their own towns, in which each merchant or craft guild was assigned a sector of the walls to man. Nevertheless, such militiamen sometimes took part in offensive sieges against enemy fortifications, or fought in the field army, and they were probably the first men in the Polish armies to use hand-held firearms. The townspeople were also responsible for maintaining their own city walls in defensible condition, while the serfs looked after earth-and-timber fortifications in the countryside.

Polish militia crossbowmen of the 'Cockerel Brotherhood of Cracow', illustrated in the *Codex of Belem* in around 1505. Note, left, pavises painted with images of saints; and the central crossbowman's flamboyantly parti-coloured hose. (Jagiellonian Library, Cracow)

Yet another group of combatants were the *milites stipendiarii* or mercenaries, who first appeared on a large scale during the Thirteen Years' War, though such troops had served in Polish armies at an earlier date. These mercenaries were recruited in accordance with the so-called 'companion' system which became typical of Poland. Under this system, a 'captain' was contracted by a lord or senior member of the Polish aristocracy. The captain in turn appointed his 'companions' who were, in effect, his officers. These officers then recruited, bringing with them their own attendants, including horse or foot.

Polish mercenary cavalry units were organized in much the same manner as the troops who formed part of the levy, and similarly consisted almost entirely of knights and crossbowmen. Consequently, their units were classified as being heavy or light depending on the proportion of heavy to light horsemen in each. By contrast, the Polish mercenary infantry differed from many of its Western counterparts, being made up largely of crossbowmen sheltering behind pavises and protected against the cavalry by fully armoured pikemen. Before being accepted into service, each of these mercenary units was inspected by a royal officer at the *popis* or review, to assess their suitability for combat.

In later years these crossbowmen were gradually replaced by hand-gunners. The first confirmed reference to Polish firearms dates from 1383, though such weapons may have been in use even earlier. The subsequent reign of King Wladyslaw II Jagiello (1386–1434) was the period that witnessed the most rapid development of gunpowder artillery in Poland, but it was the Thirteen Years' War of the 1450s–60s against the Teutonic Knights which really saw firearms come into their own, not only in siege and field operations but also in naval warfare. The artillery personnel in Polish armies included the usual three groups of specialists: the 'gunner-tacticians' who operated cannon in the field, the 'gunner-

Detail from an oil painting of the battle of Orsha in 1514, made only 15 or 20 years after the event. Several details are discussed in the commentaries to Plate H. Note, foreground, the Polish-Lithuanian artillery crossing a bridge of boats followed by heavily armoured infantrymen. (National Museum, Warsaw)

technicians' who produced artillery equipment and ammunition, and the 'universal gunners', who were skilled in both these discipines. Most such men were drawn from the urban population, but there were also gunners of noble origin in later medieval Poland.

The second half of the 15th century witnessed a noticeable decline in effectiveness of the existing Polish military system. This was partly a result of social changes within the kingdom: the nobility who had evolved from a knighthood into a landed aristocracy now began to see their military duties as a begrudged necessity rather than a welcome or honourable duty. Consequently, the levy of knights which proved its effectiveness during the Thirteen Years' War was gradually replaced by more reliable and more professional mercenary troops. In 1479 an attempt to raise and maintain a permanent army alongside these temporary mercenaries resulted in the creation of the 'common defence'. These new troops, though never available in sufficient numbers, were given the task of protecting Poland's south-eastern frontiers against the Khanate of Krim or Crimean Tartars, who were allied with – and eventually vassals of – the Ottoman Turkish sultans.

A consequent problem that came to the surface around this time was that of raising sufficient taxes to pay and equip these new armies. It would never be adequately solved; the Polish nobility, though no longer themselves an effective military force, often refused to be taxed for this purpose. Given these difficulties it is hardly surprising that Polish military finances remained unstable as well as very limited. As a result, the actual size of Polish armies during the period probably varied a great deal. The largest is likely to have been the *expeditio generalis* that defeated the Teutonic Knights in 1410, with a potential maximum estimated at 36,000 cavalrymen; the Polish army that actually fought at Tannenberg/Grunwald may have numbered as many as 18,000 to 20,000 combatants. The largest known mercenary army was that raised for the war against Hungary in 1471, which consisted of 21,000 troops, including both horse and foot.

The response to the Eastern threat

Polish cavalry forces underwent the most noticeable and dramatic changes in their organization and armament during the early 16th century. Now facing more mobile and often elusive enemies such as the Crimean Tartars, Polish-Lithuanian cavalry were forced to adopt some of their enemies' tactics as well as several aspects of their arms and armour. As a consequence, mounted and to some extent infantry crossbowmen were replaced by mounted archers, this change being particularly noticeable from around

1521 onwards. The numbers of light cavalry also increased dramatically. One of several likely models for this development were those light *hussars* of Serbian origin who had first appeared in the Hungarian army of King Matthias Corvinus (the Serbian word *gussar* meaning bandit or robber).

In spite of their introduction into the Polish-Lithuanian army at the start of the 16th century, and the overall increase in the numbers of such light cavalry, heavily armoured knights or men-at-arms continued to serve and to prove their effectiveness in many encounters, especially where heavy and light cavalry operated in mutual support. In fact, within the resulting 'heavy cavalry banner', the most common proportion of hussars to archers plus men-at-arms was roughly one-to-one. This was similar to the 'light banners', though in these the mounted archers predominated over the armoured men-at-arms. Consequently, Polish cavalry units of this period were classified as *gravioris et levioris armaturae* – 'heavily and lightly armoured'.

Military contacts with the nomadic peoples of the southern Russian and now eastern Ukrainian steppes were probably a key factor in the creation of what came to be known as 'the Old Polish Array', as used by these assorted cavalry forces. This was a highly adaptable and manoeuvrable formation consisting of three main elements. The first of these was the *Vorhut* or vanguard, which was normally made up of men-at-arms and/or hussars; such a vanguard was traditionally flanked by light cavalry banners consisting of horse archers or cossacks. Second was the *Gewalthut* or centre, consisting either of heavy cavalry men-at-arms or lighter hussars. All the units of the formation could be used either en masse – and this was more typically the case – or separately, this being more normally the role of the light cavalry. A third element consisted of the remaining troops, largely infantry and artillery, who were supposed to co-operate with the cavalry depending upon events. A particularly good example of the successful use of this 'Old Polish Array' in open battle was at Obertyn. Here, next to the River Dniester in what is now the Ukraine on 22 September 1531, the Polish army faced that of the Moldavian Prince Petru Rares; the result was a comprehensive Polish victory, and the subsequent Polish reconquest of the province of Pokutia.

ARMS AND ARMOUR

**'Guards at the Holy Sepulchre',
in a miniature illustration in
the *Psalterium Nocturnum*,
made around 1220. Note the
'great helm' at left, and the
two hauberks with exposed
mail coifs. (Ecclesiastical
Library, Trzebnica)**

The Early Period: 10th–12th centuries

A shortage of archaeological evidence means that the appearance of early Polish warriors can only be reconstructed by seeking parallels and analogies in neighbouring countries, especially from the territories of what had been the Great Moravian Empire. It is clear, however, that the great majority of

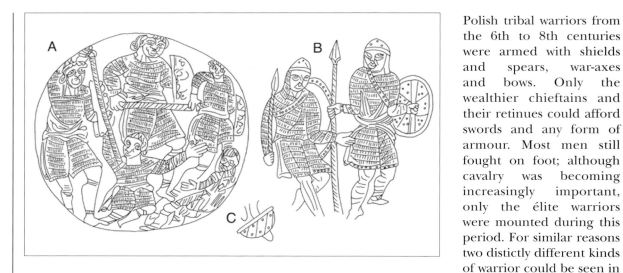

Polish tribal warriors from the 6th to 8th centuries were armed with shields and spears, war-axes and bows. Only the wealthier chieftains and their retinues could afford swords and any form of armour. Most men still fought on foot; although cavalry was becoming increasingly important, only the élite warriors were mounted during this period. For similar reasons two distictly different kinds of warrior could be seen in Polish armies of the subsequent 10th to 12th centuries. The first and less numerous group were referred to in Latin records as *loricati*; these largely consisted of horsemen wearing a helmet and mail shirt and armed with a shield, spear and sword, sometimes supplemented by a war-axe and a bow. A member of the second and far more numerous group of fighting men was known as a *clipeatus* or shield-bearer. He would almost invariably be a foot soldier armed with a spear, a battle-axe and a bow, though sometimes also possessing a sword. The increasing use of swords amongst at least a minority of non-élite warriors was a clear sign of Poland's increasing prosperity and its trading contacts.

During the period under consideration two very different forms of **helmet** were in use, both being well known to us from the archaeological record. The first was what used to be known as the 'Great Polish' style, which in fact had obvious Eastern origins and tended to be richly ornamented. Such helmets had a tall, approximately conical skull made up of four directly riveted iron pieces which were usually either gilded

Repoussé decorations on the Wlockawek Cup, Polish, 11th or early 12th century. (Archaeological Museum, Warsaw): (A) 'Israelites slaugh-tering Philistines or other foes'; (B) 'The Story of Gideon'; (C) a shield shown from the side in another biblical scene.

(Left) A directly riveted helmet – i.e. the segments are riveted to one another, not to a separate frame – found at Gorzuchy in the province of Kalisz and probably dating from the 10th or 11th century; such so-called 'Great Polish' pieces show a distinctly Eastern style.

(Right) One-piece conical helmet with a nasal, found in Lake Orchowskie in the province of Bydgoszcz; 11th to 12th century. (National Museum, Cracow; and S. Pijanowski Collection, Glucha Puszcza)

or covered with gilded copper sheet. The skull, which lacked a frame, was surmounted by a socket for a tuft of horsehair or a plume of feathers, while the sides were decorated with rosettes. The lower edge of the skull might be reinforced with a hoop joined above the forehead, and adorned with a characteristic decoration so that it resembled a diadem. From the rim hung an aventail, probably of mail, originally fastened to the hoop to protect the neck and part of the face.

In western Poland, also known as Great Poland, as many as four almost identical helmets of this type have been found. Other very similar examples come from neighbouring territories, including two from what was formerly West Prussia, one from Hungary and at least two from western Russia. The Liverpool Museum in England owns another example, which is currently on loan to the Royal Armouries in Leeds. More recent research suggests that helmets of this type were ultimately derived from an Eastern or Sassanian Iranian form, which then developed further in Russia from the 10th to the 13th centuries. During this period the style also spread westwards to Poland and Hungary. Nevertheless, the surprisingly large number of such helmets that have been unearthed in the region of Great Poland strongly suggests that there might have been a centre of production in this region, at least during the 11th century.

The second or so-called 'Norman' type of early medieval helmet is represented in Poland by two examples excavated from the Lednickie and Orchowskie lakes. They are conical helmets, forged from a single piece of iron, undecorated and, in both the Polish examples, furnished with a nasal guard. The Lednickie example has its nasal terminating in a small hook; this was almost certainly to support the mail ventail of the mail coif, and thus to provide better facial protection. Despite being representatives of a very widespread Western European form, both surviving Polish examples may well have been made locally. There is also some pictorial or artistic evidence that the framed and segmented *spangenhelm* was used in early medieval Poland, though no examples have yet been found.

Undoubtedly The **shield** was the single most important defensive item, and was probably used by all classes of warriors. Unfortunately, not a single specimen has survived in Poland – not even fragments which could serve as a basis for reconstruction. Consequently the historian has to rely on written reference to the shields in medieval Polish sources, and on similar objects from neighbouring countries. The earliest pictorial source is a depiction on *denars*, or coins, from the reign of Boleslaw II the Bold and dating from around 1058–79; these feature a horseman carrying a large kite-shaped shield plus a lance with a pennon. While it is possible that these *denars* are merely unmodified copies of a German coin form, they might also be taken as reasonably reliable evidence for the use of this elongated shield in mid- or late

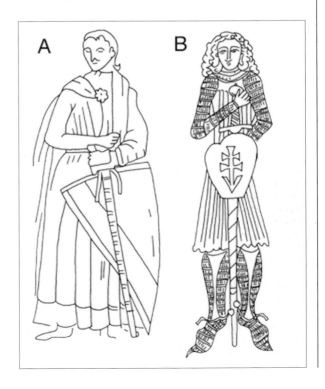

Polish effigial monuments from the age of mail:
(A) An 18th-century drawing of the since-lost carved tomb of Piotr Vlast, c.1270, which used to be in the Vinzenkloster Church in Wroclaw. (Ms. IV, f.239, University Library, Wroclaw)
(B) The incised effigial slab of Pakoslaw Lis of Mstyczów, the castellan of Cracow, c.1319; again, note the distinctively Central European shield blazon – see Plate D2. (*in situ* parish church, Jedrzejów)

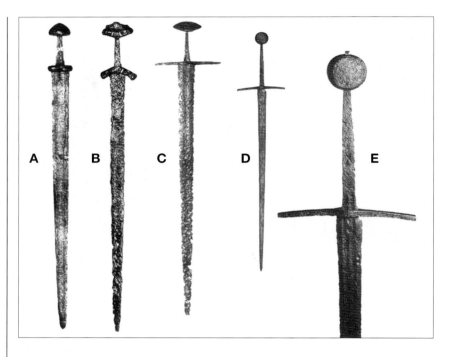

Swords found in Poland:

(A) 9th–10th century, found at Machów; **(B)** 11th century, found at Brzesc Kujawski; **(C)** 11th century, found at Psary; **(D & E)** 14th-century sword found at Michrów.

11th-century Poland. Other sources strongly suggest that a more archaic circular form of shield continued to be used, however.

The **mail hauberk** was almost certainly the most common form of body armour in Poland from the 10th to 12th centuries, as it was in the country's Western neighbours. Once again it is unfortunate that no authentic example has been preserved in Poland, though there are several references to such hauberks in the written records. Even though we can assume that the mail hauberk was the most popular or widespread type of armour, we cannot reject the possibility that other forms were also in use. For example, some wealthier warriors may have worn, in addition to their mail, lamellar or perhaps even scale armour obtained through peaceful or warlike contacts with neighbouring countries, especially those to the east and south-east.

Most of the early medieval **swords** found within Poland's borders date from the period between 950 and 1100. There are about 90 examples that fall within those types considered characteristic of Northern, Western and Central Europe. We can identify swords of the following types, as classified by Petersen: B, D, H, I, K, M, R, S, T, X, Y, and Z.[1] A particularly fine sword of Petersen's type T found at Czersko Polskie was especially interesting: its quillons and pommel were carved from horn and had probably been mounted on the blade in Poland. However, the majority of those swords that can be considered as locally made belong to Petersen's type X. There are also swords classified in Polish sources as belonging to type 'alfa', which were fitted with almond-shaped pommels and seem to have been popular from the early 10th to the late 12th centuries. The evidence indicates that the **sabre**, which was regarded as the typical weapon of the nomads of the Eurasian steppes, was popular in Hungary and well known in Russia but was not common in early medieval Poland.

As to the scabbard or sheath which was necessary for any sort of bladed sidearm, a few examples or fragments have been found in Poland. One specimen was discovered in an archaeological stratum in the city of Gdansk that has been identified as 11th century. This scabbard was made from two slender pieces of wood, covered with canvas and horsehide; its overall length was 78cm, with a maximum width of 6.5cm (30.7in by 2.5 inches). Other examples show that the lower end was sometimes furnished with a chape of ornamented

1 J.Petersen, *De Norske Vikingesvaerd* (Oslo, 1919)

bronze; but this form of decoration was rare, and may have been imported from outside Poland.

In early feudal Poland the sword remained an expensive weapon, normally possessed only by the wealthier noblemen or professional warriors from a prince's *druzhina*. A much more common weapon during this period was the **war-axe**, which was sometimes fitted to a long shaft. In addition to simple axe-heads with flat backs, another more specialized type, with a spike or hammer on the side facing away from the blade, was

(Left) Two axeheads dating from the early 11th century, found in the cemetery at Lutomiersk. (Centre for the Archaeology of Central Poland, Lodz) (Right) Bronze macehead found at Gorzyce, and believed to date from the 12th or 13th century.

also used. Some blades were symmetrical, a style having a 'beard' or downwards extension apparently being the most popular in Poland; axes with more asymmetrical blades, comparable to the archetypal 'Viking' form, were rare, and most were probably imported. Examples decoratively inlaid with non-ferrous metals were similarly exceptional. It should always be borne in mind that in cases of emergency ordinary carpenter's or agricultural axes were certainly employed as weapons.

The **spear** was used by cavalry and foot-soldiers alike, both for throwing and for hand-to-hand thrusting; during this period there was less of a clear distinction between spears and javelins in Poland than in some other countries. Amongst the surviving spearheads are some with a rather broad, lancet-like or leaf-shaped head; but examples with a more massive blade, rhomboid in section, clearly predominate. These features were the result of the need to adapt earlier styles of spearhead so that they could pierce shields or mail hauberks, such 'armour-piercing' blades gradually becoming more widespread. The spear-shafts were usually about 2m (78in) in length, as indicated by the remains found in warrior burials (some of which still included weapons as late as the 12th century in Poland). Generally speaking, locally made spearheads – like axeheads – remained undecorated, and the few exceptions, some of which were inlaid with silver, should probably be regarded as imports, usually from Scandinavia. A number of so-called 'winged' spearheads, with lateral lugs below their blades, have also been found in Poland; by contrast, these were probably imported from Germany.

The **bow**, which was widely used by foot soldiers, clearly played an important part in early medieval Polish warfare. Fragments of an almost straight bow of simple wooden construction were found in Cracow, and this specimen from Wawel Hill may originally have been about 180cm (71in) long, the largest surviving fragment measuring 65cm (25.6 inches). However, one might assume that the composite bow was also known in at least some part of early medieval Poland.

If this was the case, then such weapons were probably introduced through contacts with Russia and the steppe nomads from north of the Black Sea. By the second half of the 12th century, however, the crossbow became more widespread in Poland, as indicated by the remarkably large numbers of crossbow bolts and boltheads that have been found during archaeological excavations.

Along with the weapons mentioned above, a few **mace** heads of quite sophisticated cast construction have been found, these probably having been imported from Russia. Most of them belong to types III and IV, according to Kirpitchnikov's classification.[2] The extraordinary examples of a *scramasax* or *langsax* which have also been found would appear to be interesting exeptions rather than remotely typical of early medieval Polish weaponry.

The Middle Period: 12th–14th centuries

The era of Polish history known as the Division in the Provinces, from 1138 until 1320, was marked by a distinct predominance of Western influences upon Polish military equipment – an influence that would continue until the middle of the 16th century. We have a varied assortment of iconographic or pictorial sources for information about Polish arms and armour in this period; these include the official seals of the Piast dukes and rulers, effigies, carved slabs and engraved brasses, religious art and other forms of miniature painting. The overall impression obtained from these sources does not differ very much from what could be seen in France or England, and was even more similar to neighbouring Bohemia and Germany. Surviving pieces of military equipment from the period are, however, extremely rare.

Among the few surviving weapons, **swords** are once again the most numerous, and about 50 examples have been found in Poland dating from the 12th to 13th centuries. These fall within Oakeshott's types XI, XII, XIII and XIIIa.[3] Swords of Oakeshott's type XI appeared as early as the 11th century and remained in use until the end of the 13th century. They are all single-handed weapons with disc pommels and straight crossguards; their pointed blades, which were intended for both cut and thrust, have a narrow fuller which extends up to 80 per cent of the blade's overall length. On the other hand, swords of type XII seem to be the most common in Poland from the early 13th century to the first quarter of the 14th century. Their thrusting blades had a maximum length of 80cm (31.5in), while the fuller reaches up to 75 per cent of the

2 A.Kirpitchnikov, *Drevnerusskoe Oruzhie* (Leningrad, 1971)
3 E.Oakeshott, *Records of the Medieval Sword* (Woolbridge, 1991)

Images from 13th-century Polish seals:
(A) Seal of Prince Leskek 'the White', 1220
(B) Seal of Prince Ziemovit of Mazovia, before 1262
(C) Seal of Duke Boleslaw II 'the Bald' of Liegnitz
(D) Seal of Prince Konrad of Mazovia, 1200–25.

24

(continued on page 33)

THE LATE 10th-11th CENTURIES
1: Western Polish duke, 11th century
2: Eastern Polish warrior, late 10th century
3: Eastern Polish *voivode*, late 11th century

A

THE 12th CENTURY
1: *Loricatus*, late 12th century
2: Eastern Polish infantryman, early 12th century
3 & 4: Man and woman of rural elite, mid-12th century

B

THE 13th CENTURY
1: Silesian knight in service of Piast dynasty, mid-13th century
2: Brother knight of Order of Dobrzyn, early 13th century
3: Eastern Polish infantryman, late 13th century

FIRST HALF OF THE 14th CENTURY
1: Mazovian nobleman, mid-14th century
2: Southern Polish knight, early 14th century
3: Western Polish knight of Buzewoj family, early 14th century

D

SECOND HALF OF THE 14th CENTURY
1: Nobleman, late 14th century
2: Northern Polish knight in service of Lord of Sieradz, mid-14th century
3: Crossbowman, late 14th century

E

FIRST HALF OF THE 15th CENTURY
1: Man-at-arms in service of Strasy of Odroway and Bialaczow, early 15th century
2: Wealthy burgher, mid-15th century
3: Hand-gunner, mid-15th century

F

SECOND HALF OF THE 15th CENTURY
1: Man-at-arms, mid- to late 15th century
2: Eastern Polish light cavalryman, late 15th century
3: Mercenary crossbowman, late 15th century

G

EARLY 16th CENTURY
1: Army commander, early 16th century
2: Hussar, c.1520
3: Man-at-arms, early 16th century

H

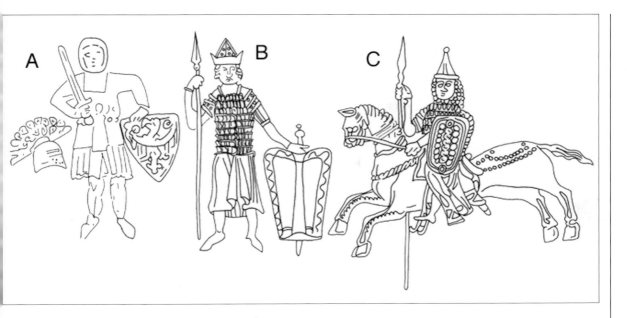

Images from 14th-century Polish seals:
(A) Seal of Duke Bernard of Schweidnitz, c.1307–25
(B) Seal of the Duke of Mazovia, 1343
(C) Seal of Duke Trojden of Mazovia, attached to a document of 1341

length. Examples of type XIII and XIIIa weapons could be regarded as the heavy 'swords of war', and were also characteristic of Scandinavia, Germany and Central Europe. They appeared in Poland during the 13th century and remained in use until the end of the medieval period. Here the fuller usually reached the middle of the massive blade, which was itself sometimes more than 110cm (43.3in) long. Although there are no surviving examples, pictorial sources suggest that some forms of dagger were also used by Polish knights of these centuries.

The evidence indicates that the more specialized cavalry lance, rather than the earlier and simpler spear, also became popular in Poland as early as the 12th century. For example, the seal of Duke Mieszko III the Old, dated between 1173 and 1202, clearly depicts a horseman wielding such a lance. Nevertheless, older types of spear do seem to have remained in use simultaneously. Unfortunately the lack of surviving original examples means that we have to rely upon pictorial sources to provide an admittedly rather poor idea of the sorts of **polearm** used by Polish infantry. Weapons such as the halberd, poleaxe, glaive and bardiche do not seem to have been widespread, though one cannot rule out their use, while axes and maces, though again poorly documented, may occasionally have been used.

The bow remained in use throughout the medieval period, but it was the **crossbow** that became more common during these centuries. In medieval Poland this kind of missile weapon first appeared during the second half of the 12th century, and became much more widespread during the 13th century. For example, Duke Bolko I of Schweidnitz/ Swidnica was credited with recruiting crossbowmen into his household troops as early as 1286. The earliest fragments of crossbows or of boltheads that have been discovered in Poland similarly date from the 13th century.

According to Claude Blair, the period from 1066 to 1250 is commonly defined as 'The Age of Mail'. Clearly, mail armour did remain the main form of protection amongst Polish men-at-arms, though it also went through a number of significant changes or improvements. The first

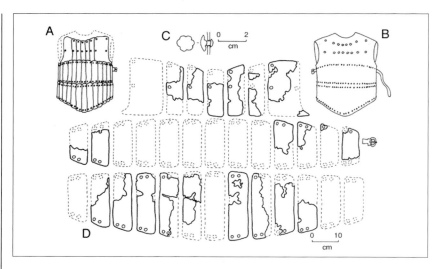

Coat-of-plates from the castle of Plemieta, which was burned down in 1414:
(A) Reconstruction of the iron scales assembled, seen from inside without the fabric covering
(B) Reconstruction of the complete armour with its fabric covering and leather strap
(C) Detail of one of the rosette-shaped rivets
(D) Surviving fragments of the iron scales, with complete set indicated by dotted lines.
(Provincial Museum, Grudziadz)

evidence for more rigid or semi-rigid armours in Poland again dates from the 13th century. The earliest reference to a **coat-of-plates** comes from the first half of that century, while the seal of Duke Henry II the Pious (c.1228–34) certainly shows a knight wearing a simple form of such armour. Another seal depicting the coat-of-plates is that of Duke Bernard of Schweidnitz, dating from between 1307 and 1325. Some forms of early **leg defence**, such as poleyns and schynbalds, can be seen on the incised tomb-slab of Pakoslaw of Mstyczów, which was made around 1319 (see page 21).

Another dramatic change during this period was the introduction of the 'great helm'. The seal of Duke Casimir I of Kuyavia, c.1236, is the earliest evidence for the 'great helm' in Poland, but there is no reason to suppose that such helmets were not worn a generation or so earlier by some cavalrymen. The reason for their development was probably connected with the introduction of the armour-piercing cavalry lance; this form obviously offered better face protection during a frontal charge. On the other hand, several different forms of helmet clearly remained in use in Poland – as elsewhere – throughout this period alongside the all-enclosing great helm; rounded and cylindrical styles, with or without nasals, also remained popular. The brimmed war-hat or *chapel-de-fer* may similarly have been worn, as well as the older conical helmets, but unfortunately there are no surviving examples.

The Later Period: 14th–16th centuries

The next period, from c.1334 to c.1500, was characterized by further Westernization of Polish armies, their arms and their armour. However, there was one particularly interesting exception to this general trend. The knights or élite cavalry in Mazovia in north-eastern Poland appeared distinctly different, and remarkably similar to their Russian or Lithuanian neighbours and adversaries. These Eastern features were clearly depicted in numerous seals that were made for the dukes of Mazovia between 1228 and 1334. One seal of Duke Trojden I, dating from 1341 (see page 33), featured a mounted warrior wearing a tall conical helmet and a lamellar cuirass of seemingly entirely Eastern or Asiatic style. He is armed with a spear, and carries a similarly distinctive so-called 'small Lithuanian pavise'; this form of shield was otherwise used by (and indeed highly characteristic of) the pagan Baltic peoples, but its unmistakable form had already appeared as early as 1228 on the seal of Duke Conrad I of Mazovia. It was nearly rectangular in outline, and had a vertical keel or corrugation protruding from the front. Somewhat later surviving examples from the Czech Republic range from approximately 60cm to 80cm (24–31 inches) in vertical length.

Further developments in the **armour** of 14th century Poland can be traced in considerable detail from the monumental effigies of the Silesian Piast rulers. The effigy of Duke Bolko I of Schweidnitz, dating from around 1301, shows some form of vertically quilted soft armour beneath the duke's mail armour (see page 43). The effigy also depicts a 'great helm', adorned with a double crest of feathers. Several further items can be seen on the dual effigy of Duke Bolko II and his wife from around 1341–42 (see page 11); the duke is equipped with plated knee and leg defences, and wears a breastplate and gauntlets. A fabric-covered breastplate with a retaining chain to a sword is represented on the effigy of Bolko III, c.1380 (see page 45); this also includes plated leg and arm defences, and a crested helm.

Of perhaps even greater significance are the 400-odd metal fragments of what had been a coat-of-plates which were found in Nowe Miasto on the Warta river. Once reassembled, they provide a very clear impression of how a 14th-century body armour from this part of Central Europe originally looked. Some other fragments of plate armour, this time dated around 1386, have also been discovered along with a helmet in Siedlatków on the Warta. This helmet is a bascinet, with a rounded visor attached to the brow of the skull by a bar and hinge. Another supposedly 'egg-shaped' basinet was found in Sandomierz, apparently dating from the 1350s to 1370s; that example probably belonged to King Casimir the Great himself, having been fitted with a folding crown and removable 'nasal-visor'. Amongst the other interesting items found more recently in southern Poland is a fragment of the domed upper part of a 'great helm', remarkably similar to that which belonged the Black Prince of England and which has been dated at around 1376.

(A–G) Spear and javelin blades from the ruined castle of Chelminski, 13th–14th century. (after A. Nadolski)
(H–K) Elements in the manufacture of a 14th- or 15th-century Polish crossbow bolt: **(H)** basic shaft, **(I)** shaft with end shaved to accept bolthead, **(J)** shaft with wooden flights attached, **(K)** iron bolthead, **(L)** completed bolt.
(M–Q) Nomad-style broad arrowheads from Piemieta, 13th–14th centuries. (after A. Nadolski)

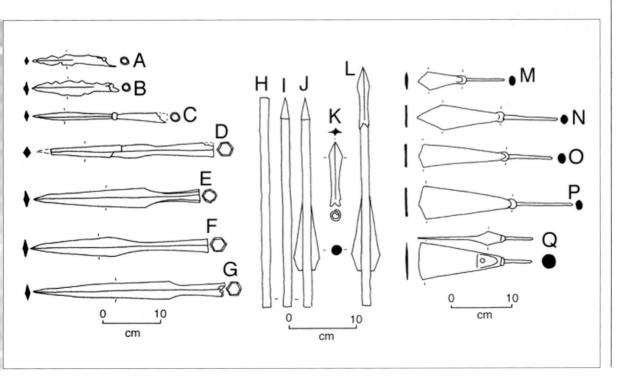

Gauntlets of what is sometimes called the 'hourglass' form may have been used in Poland; several small metal elements have been found which closely resemble a surviving gauntlet from Orum in Denmark. This particular style seems to have been popular during the late 14th and early 15th centuries; this provides further evidence that mid-14th-century Polish armourers were now beginning to keep up with the rest of Catholic Central and Western Europe.

Judging by the pictorial evidence, fully developed 'white harness' or armour of uncovered steel plates had reached Poland by about 1425. This was approximately when the effigial slab and memorial painting of Wierzbiêta of Branice were made (see page 12); they illustrate a knight clad in such *alwite* armour, complete with a visored basinet. Nevertheless, the fauld on these particular cuirasses seems to be covered in fabric. Another type of armour which appears in Polish pictorial sources is specifically German in style, incorporating a vertically fluted, almost box-shaped breastplate or *kastenbrust*. One characteristic feature of such armour was a particularly deep fauld, as can clearly be seen in the memorial painting of Jan of Ujazd, c. 1450 (see page 14). The brass of Jan Koniecpolski and his sons, from around 25 years later, shows knights wearing yet another style of full armour which is considered to have originated in southern Germany; interestingly, this notably angular type of armour has its breastplate radially fluted, with its lower part protruding forwards (see page 15).

There is no clear evidence that armours of Italian manufacture or style were ever widespread in 15th-century Poland; and German armours of the fully developed so-called 'Gothic' form reached Poland no earlier than 1475. A particularly magnificent armour, complete with bevor and sallet, appeared on the brass of Lukasz of Górka, c.1488 (see page 5). Though there are some references to the use of horse armour this probably never

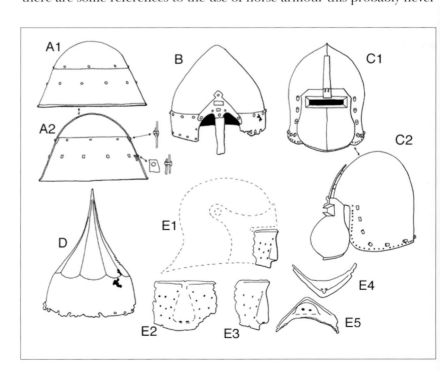

(A) Reconstructions of a crushed iron 'war-hat' from the castle of Plemieta, so no later than 1414: (A1) exterior, (A2) section and interior, showing riveting system and attachment points for a lining. (Provincial Museum, Grudziadz)
(B) Helmet perhaps remade from an earlier conical helmet, considered by Dr Michael Gorelik to be late 13th or early 14th century. (National Museum, Cracow)
(C) Reconstruction of a bascinet with a 'pig-faced' visor found at Siedlatków, in the remains of a castle that was burned down in 1382–83: (C1) front, (C2) side. (National Archaeological Museum, Lodz)
(D) One-piece helmet of probable Russian origin, late 14th or early 15th century, found in the River Pregola in north-eastern Poland; present location unknown.
(E) Fragment of the visor from a sallet, from a fortified manor-house at Spytkowice in southern Poland, late 15th century: (E1) Reconstruction of entire helmet, (E2) visor fragment from front, (E3) visor fragment from side, (E4) visor fragment from above, (E5) visor fragment from below. (Archaeological Institute, Cracow)

became widespread in 15th-century Poland. Pictorial evidence suggests that this changed during the early 16th century, especially with the introduction of armours of the 'Maximilian' style.

Meanwhile, despite all the technological and stylistic innovations described above, including a rise in the use of hand-held firearms, the **sword** remained the main offensive weapon throughout this later period. The 33 swords that are known to have survived from the mid-14th to late 15th centuries belong to the following types in Oakeshott's classifications: XVIa (15 examples), XVII (14), XIIIa (1), and XX (3 examples). Swords of type XVIa have long blades with a fuller, are hexagonal in section, and have a two-handed hilt with a straight crossguard and a massive disc-shaped pommel. The blades of type XVII are hexagonal and octagonal in section in their upper and lower parts respectively; despite their obvious cutting capabilities, swords of this type were intended primarily for thrusting. The overall length of type XX swords is more than 150cm (59in); their broad, flat blades, with double or even triple fullers, were intended mainly for cuts rather than thrusts. The hilts of types XVII and XX are both two-handed, with straight, massive crossguards and pommels.

Another kind of weapon used in Poland at this time was the *estoc* or *tuck* – a form of thrusting sword with a long, stiff blade, square or rhomboid in section. *Estoc* fighting techniques relied upon thrusting attacks aimed at those parts of the opponent where his armour was weakest or even absent. There are two surviving examples in Poland, dated from the 14th and 15th centuries, one of them measuring more than 90cm (35.4in) long. Used largely by cavalrymen, such an *estoc* was normally carried on the saddle.

Details from a superb Polish bas-relief carving of the 'Guards at the Holy Sepulchre', made by Wit Stwosz of Nurnberg between 1477 and 1489. As so often, this much-depicted New Testament scene is a precious gift to researchers of medieval military equipment. Note (left) the decorative inner borders on the visor of the sallet, the bevor and the cuffs of the gauntlets; and the fluting effect on the arm harness of both figures – see commentary to Plate G1. (*in situ* Church of St Mary the Virgin, Cracow)

After being effectively unknown in medieval Poland, the **sabre** quite suddenly became more widespread during the second half of the 15th century, and is mentioned as early as 1464. Because it had a more universal application than the medieval knightly sword, the sabre became increasingly popular amongst both infantry and light cavalry. Early sabres of what could be regarded as Turco-Hungarian style or origin now appeared in art quite frequently, but not one original example from this period has yet been found. Instead, the sabre excavated from the Narew near Pultusk has a hilt much like that of a normal straight sword, with a straight crossguard; even the blade, though slightly curved, is still pointed.

The **falchion** was another kind of sidearm that became more widespread during this period, though again it might have been known even earlier. Polish-made falchions seem to have been relatively inexpensive while still of high quality, and consequently such weapons grew in popularity amongst all classes of fighting men.

Daggers came in a variety of forms, and from the 13th to 15th centuries became an indispensable piece of knightly equipment. Generally speaking the form of a dagger blade was closely related to current development of the plate armour which such weapons were intended to penetrate or bypass, and daggers found in Poland seem to follow the most common patterns seen elsewhere. A so-called 'ballock dagger' typical of the 14th century, with its triangular blade clearly indicated, is depicted on the effigy of King Casimir the Great, which was made between 1370 and 1380. The 15th-century form known as the 'rondel dagger', with a blade of rhomboid section, was also in use. As can be seen in the pictorial sources, dagger attacks were mainly aimed at the eye-slits in an opponent's helmet or at his relatively unprotected neck.

Another detail from the painting of the battle of Orsha, made in the first third of the 16th century. This depicts a group of Polish or Lithuanian light cavalry hussars approaching the River Dnieper, and clearly shows the braided costume and unusual headgear reconstructed in Plate H2. (National Museum, Warsaw)

The **war-hammer** remained a practical weapon, whereas the mace gradually evolved into an insignia of office rather than a tool of war. Amongst staff weapons the **pike**, though never as popular in Poland as it was among Swiss or German mercenaries, did play a role. Its function was, however, primarily defensive, which limited its acceptance amongst the tactically offensive and largely 'missile-armed' Polish foot soldiers, whose basic infantry unit was usually made up of one pikeman, one pavise- or shield-bearer, and seven hand-gunners or crossbowmen. Most commonly used by foot soldiers, the **war-flail** was probably introduced by the Bohemian Hussites who served in considerable numbers in the armies of both Poland and the Teutonic Knights, especially during the mid-15th century.

Newly formed units of light cavalrymen were armed with a lightened '**hussar lance**' along with their equally characteristic sabre. Such light cavalry also carried an asymmetrical, pointed shield that was probably of Turco-Hungarian origin, though round forms also remained in use.

Firearms, while first mentioned in the 1380s, did not appear in substantial numbers until the 15th century. As in the rest of Europe, cannon came in a great variety of calibres and barrel-lengths. Following his unsuccessful campaign of 1497, Jan Olbracht is said to have left about 40 different pieces of artillery in Lwów. It was in 1506 that mobile field artillery was first mentioned as being employed by Polish troops, at the battle of Kleck. Meanwhile, hand-held firearms probably appeared in Poland at around the same time as they did elsewhere, though again they did not became widespread until the mid-15th century, and they did not entirely replace the crossbow as a war-weapon until 1522.

Detail of effigial brass of Piotr Kmita, the *voivode* of Cracow, dating from around 1505; this was made by Peter Vischer of Nurnberg. Note the hairstyle; the unarmoured inside of his right thigh; the lance, and the two two-handed swords depicted. The blazon of a small cross rising from a 'reversed S' motif can be seen on his banner and on the shield at his feet; compare with earlier painting of Jan of Ujazd on page 14. (*in situ* Cathedral, Cracow)

SELECT BIBLIOGRAPHY

Byrne, B., 'The Spurs of King Casimir III and some other Fourteenth Century Spurs', *Journal of the Arms and Armour Society*, 3 (1959–61), 106–115

Chodynski, A.R., 'The Significance of the Lost Painting, The Siege of Malbork in 1460, from Dvór Artusa in the Study of the Arms and Armour of the Close of the Fifteenth Century', in W. Swietoslawski (ed.), *Warfare in the Middle Ages: Acta Archaeologica Lodziensia*, 47 (Lódz, 2001), 83–99

Christiansen, E., *The Northern Crusades: The Baltic and Catholic Frontier 1100–1525* (London, 1980)

De Markov, D.D., 'The Battle of Tannenberg (Grunwald) in 1410' in (anon ed) *From Crécy to Mohacs: Warfare in the Late Middle Ages* (London, 1997), 300–305

Deveike, J., 'The Lithuanian Diarchies', *The Slavonic and Eastern European Review*, 28 (1949–50)

Golinski, M., 'Some remarks on the issue of the tactical organization of knight forces (an addition to the recent history of Poland)', in W. Swietoslawski (ed), *Warfare in the Middle Ages: Acta Archaeologica Lodziensia*, 47 (Lódz, 2001) 67–70

Grabarczyk, T., *Piechota zaciezna Królestwa Polskiego w XV wieku* (Lódz, 2000); (English summary) 'Infantry hired by the Polish Kingdom in the Fifteenth Century', 301–307

The dramatic setting of the castle of Chojnik, which dates from the 14th to 16th centuries; it was built for the ukes of Schweidnitz-Jawor.

Halecki, O., *Borderlands of Western Civilization: A History of East Central Europe* (New York, 1952)

Herrmann, J., 'The Northern Slavs', in D.M. Wilson (ed), *The Northern World* (London, 1980)

Heymowski, A., 'Les chevaliers polonais de l'époque de Louis le Grand representés dans l'Armorial Bellenville', in S.B. Vardy (ed), *Louis the Great, King of Hungary and Poland* (New York, 1986), 140–174

Iwanczak, W., 'The Pretended Miracle or the Battle of Chlumec in 1126', in W. Swietoslawski (ed), *Warfare in the Middle Ages: Acta Archaeologica Lodziensia*, 47 (Lódz, 2001), 12–18

Kajzer, L., *Uzbrojenie i ubiór rycerski w sredniowiecznej Malopolsce w swietle zródel ikonograficznych* (Wroclaw, 1976); 'Arms and Armour of the medieval Chivalry of Little Poland in the Light of Iconographic Sources', 147–149

Klein, A., Sekunda, N., & Czernielewski, K.A., *Banderia apud Grunwald; Polish banners at Grunwald* (Lódz, 2000)

Knoll, P., 'Economic and Political Institutions on the Polish-German Frontier in the Middle Ages: Action, Reaction, Interaction', in R. Bartless & A. Mackay (eds), *Medieval Frontier Societies* (Oxford, 1989), 151–174

Kola, A., & G. Wilke, 'Produkcka Grotów Beltów do Kuszny w sredniowieczu w swietle Wspólczesnych prób eksperymentalnych (Die produktion der armbrustpfeilspitzen im mittelalter im lichte der heutigen experimentierversuche)', *Acta Universitatis Nicolai Copernici: Archeologia V: Nauke Humanistyczno-Spoleczne*, 68 (Torun, 1975), 161–181

Nadolski, A., 'Ancient Polish Arms and Armour', *The Journal of the Arms and Armour Society*, 4 (London, 1962–64) 29–39, 170–186

Nadolski, A. (ed), *Uzbrojenie w Polsce sredniowiecznej 1350–1450* (Lódz, 1990); 'Arms and Armour in Medieval Poland 1350–1450', 465–481

Nadolski, A. (ed), *Polska technika wojskowa do 1500* (Warsaw, 1994); 'Polish Military Technology until 1500', 423–430

Nadolki, A., 'Szczerbiec – The Polish Coronation Sword', *Journal of the Arms and Armour Society*, 6 (1960), 183–184

Nowakowski, A., *Uzbrojenie w Polsce sredniowiecznej 1450–1500* (Torun, 1998); 'Arms and Armour in Medieval Poland 1450–1500', 322–323

Nowakowski, A., 'The battles fought by Mieszko I for Pomerania-on-Oder', in W. Swietoslawski (ed), *Warfare in the Middle Ages: Acta Archaeologica Lodziensia*, 47 (Lódz, 2001), 7–11

Ossowska, J., 'The Polish contribution to the expeditions to the Holy Land in the Crusader era', *Folia Orientalia*, 26 (1989), 166–182

Parenko, R., 'Standards of Living, Order and Prestige: Public Facilities in Early Fifteenth Century Lviv (Lemberg)', *Medium Aevum Quotidianum*, 42 (2000); first part republished on the *De Re Militari* website: www.deremilitari.org

Paszkiewicz, M., 'Polish War-Hammers: Czekan, Nadziak, Obuck', *Journal of the Arms and Armour Society*, 8 (1975), 225–228

Pierzak, J., *Sredniowieczne helmy garnczkowe na ziemiach polskich na tle zachodnioeuropejskim; Rocznik Muzeum Górnoslaskiego w Bytomiu. Archeologia*, 16 (Bytom, 2005); 'Medieval heaume in the territory of Poland as compared to Western Europe', 380–382

Stone, D., *The Polish-Lithuanian State, 1386–1795* (Washington, 2001)

Strzyz, P., 'Uzbrojenie we wzesnosredniowiecznej Malopolsce', *Acta Archaeologica Lodziensia*, 52 (Lódz, 2006); 'Weaponry in Early Medieval Malopolska', 147–149

Szymczak, J., 'Relieving a besieged city in medieval Poland', in W. Swietoslawski (ed), *Warfare in the Middle Ages: Acta Archaeologica Lodziensia*, 47 (Lódz, 2001), 37–43

Szymczak, J., *Poczatki broni palnej w Polsce 1383–1533* (Lódz, 2004); 'The Beginnings of Firearms in Poland 1383–1533', 383–388

Turska, K., *Ubior dworski w Polsce w dobie pierwszych Jagiellonów* (Wroclaw, 1987); 'Le costume de cour en Pologne sous les premiers Jagellons', 272–275

Vardy, S.B. (ed), *Louis the Great, King of Hungary and Poland* (New York, 1986)

Wawrzonowska, Z., *Uzbrojenie i ubiór rycerski Piastów slaskich od XII do XIV w.* (Lódz, 1976); 'Knightly Arms and Dress of the Silesian Piasts from the 12th to the 14th century', 47–49

Wilinbackow, W., 'Poczatkowy Okres Rozwoju Broni Palnej w Krajach Slowianskich', *Kwartalnik Historii Techniki*, 8 (1963) 215–235; 'Note on the History of the Initial Period of the Use of Firearms in the Slavonic Countries', 234–235

Woznicka-Staf, A., & Kolosowski, P., 'Découvertes templières en Pologne: Les templiers en Pologne: Chwarszczany, une commanderie au septentrional du monde chrétien; Rurka, une commanderie énigmatique', *Histoire et Images Médiévales*, 5 (Dec 2005–Jan 2006), 39–53

Zygulski, Z., 'The Battle of Orsha', in R. Held (ed), *Art, Arms and Armour: An International Anthology* (Chiasso, 1979), 108–143

Zygulski, Z., 'Knightly Arms – Plebian Arms', *Quaestiones Medii Aevi Novae*, 4 (1999); republished on the *De Re Militari* website: www.deremilitari.org

Polish fortifications, 14th–16th centuries (after Kaufmann & Kaufmann):

(A) Checiny Castle: (1) bailey, (2) moat, (3) gate tower and chapel, (4) courtyard of upper castle, (5) great hall, (6) courtyard of lower castle, (7) cistern.
(B) Olsztyn Castle: (1) curtain wall, (2) lower castle, (3) 16th-century bastion, (4) dry moat, (5) courtyard of lower castle, (6) courtyard of upper castle, (7) keep, (8) rocky outcrops.
(C) Nidzica Castle: (1) stone bridge, (2) dry moat, (3) lower castle, (4) bastions, (5) courtyard of upper castle, (6) keep.

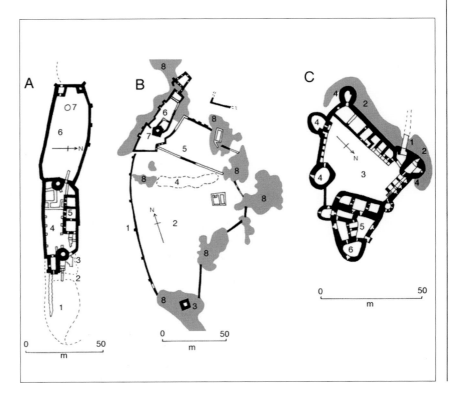

PLATE COMMENTARIES

A: THE LATE 10th–11th CENTURIES

A1: Western Polish duke, 11th century

This representative of one of the first kings receives the allegiance of an eastern Polish local leader. The duke's equipment clearly reflects the strong influence from Germany and other parts of Central Europe. He wears an early form of almost conical helmet, forged from one piece but lacking a nasal bar. His long-sleeved mail *hauberk* similarly lacks an integral mail *coif* and, being slit at the sides rather than front and back of the hem, is again of an early form primarily designed for combat on foot. It would almost certainly be worn over some kind of 'soft armour' – probably of felt rather than quilting at this date. A leather *guige* would support a round shield on his back or hip, here protected from the rain by his cloak. A plain leather sword belt is slit and tied around a leather-covered wooden scabbard; the sword is probably imported from Germany, but the quillons and pommel carved from horn would have been added locally, in imitation of a widespread Western/Central European style. The duke's other weapons are an iron axe and a long-bladed spear. While his arms and armour fall within what was becoming a 'Western' military tradition, his horse's decorated bridle still shows local Eastern European influence.

A2: Eastern Polish warrior, late 10th century

Indigenous Polish traditions are more obvious in the appearance of this local headman; note his fur-lined hat and loose trousers, and the almost tribal decoration on his oval wooden shield. The spear, with its protruding 'wings' beneath the blade, could have been seen across most of Europe, though it was by now old-fashioned by the standards of Germany and some other neighbouring Christian countries. By contrast, his decorated war-axe is distinctive, and was probably captured from the still-pagan Prussians to the north.

A3: Eastern Polish *voivode*, late 11th century

Eastern traditions and fashions, some originating as far away as the Central Asian steppes, remained strong in many of the eastern regions that would be drawn into the Kingdom of Poland. They are visible in several aspects of this regional or tribal governor's armour and clothing (though not in his sword, either imported or based upon Western/Central European forms). This segmented and highly decorated helmet was once termed the 'Great Polish' form, but is now known to have been representative of a tradition that spread across Hungary, Russia, the steppes at least as far as Central Asia, and much of the Middle East. Rather than being worn over a *coif*, it has a mail *aventail* attached to the rim. His cloak and tunic are made of costly Middle Eastern textiles. Eastern fashions are obvious in the horse's harness; the 'nomad-style' saddle has elaborate metal edging reinforcement, and, though obscured here, the bit would have large cheek-bars or *psalions*.

B: THE 12th CENTURY

As Poland expanded and its rulers consolidated their power, Polish armies found themselves fighting in very varied terrain, ranging from the huge marshes and forest of the north to the mountains which separated Poland from Bohemia, and soon also to the open, almost steppe-like country of what is now the Ukraine.

B1: *Loricatus*, late 12th century

By the late 12th century the Polish aristocracy had entirely adopted Central European styles of military equipment, though all but the wealthiest remained somewhat old-fashioned by the standards seen in Germany to the west. Here a fully armoured *loricatus*, the Polish equivalent of a knight, has a full mail *hauberk*, with an integral *coif* but still lacking mail mittens. His perhaps locally made one-piece iron helmet is distinctive in having a nasal bar terminating in an outwards 'hook', almost certainly to support a flap of mail across his mouth, chin and throat. His sword is thrust into its scabbard through a slit in the left hip of the *hauberk*, as seen in France and England over a century earlier; his legs are protected by full mail *chausses* under his long tunic. The clearest evidence of Western European influence is the heraldic motif on his kite-shaped shield and his lance pennon; such heraldry had only recently been adopted by the Polish aristocracy. The horse harness, saddle and bridle are also now fully within the Western tradition.

B2: Eastern Polish infantryman, early 12th century

This foot soldier's equipment combines Western and Eastern styles. The tall helmet of directly rivetted segments is essentially Eastern, while the mail *hauberk* with an integral *coif* – here thrown back onto his shoulders – is of a form which could be found across most of Central and Western Europe. The kite-shaped shield was more widespread by this date, being seen

Front and side views of a carved bone or ivory chess 'knight' found in Cracow, probably dating from the late 13th century; sadly, this piece was lost during World War II. See commentary to Plate C3 for discussion of the features that it displays, which are important evidence for a mixing of regional influences in the equipment used in Poland at this period.

throughout Europe, in the Byzantine Empire and even in parts of the Islamic Middle East. The hollow bronze mace-head filled with lead might be more specifically Polish or East European, while the light javelins which he carries in addition to his spear reflect a style of warfare which was now rare further west.

B3 & B4: Man and woman of the Polish rural elite, mid-12th century
The costume worn by these two figures, pointing the way in unfamiliar country for the two soldiers, is based upon a decorated floor from Wilica dated 1166–77, which offers a very rare illustration of costume during this relatively early period; the man's brooch-pin, buckle and spearhead are taken from archaeological finds. His heavy wool cloak, pinned with a gilded bronze brooch, has two distinctive extensions – symbolic ties – from the upper corners, each fitted with a bronze 'strap-end'. His tunic and the woman's dress are edged with embroidered or appliqué decoration. Note his broad spearhead with silver-inlay decoration round the socket.

C: THE 13th CENTURY
Poland was drawn into what are now known as the Northern Crusades at an early date, against pagan Prussian and other tribes of the Baltic coast; Poles also soon found themselves campaigning against fellow-Catholic Teutonic Knights as well as Orthodox Christian Russians.

C1: Silesian knight in the service of the Piast dynasty, mid-13th century
The increasingly Germanized Western Polish province of Silesia was the most economically and politically advanced in the kingdom and also provided some of the best-equipped military forces. The knight shown here is virtually indistin-guishable from his German colleagues further west. He has a flat-topped 'great helm'; his heraldic surcoat with thickly padded shoulders is worn over a long-sleeved mail *hauberk* with integral mittens; this in turn is worn over a quilted *aketon* or *gambeson*, and his legs are protected by mail *chausses* and quilted *cuisses*. His sword, spear and shield are also typical of this period generally; however, the coat-of-arms consisting of an eagle with a crescent-shaped *'kleestengel'* on its breast was distinctively Silesian and Polish.

C2: Brother knight of the Order of Dobrzyn, early 13th century
The Order of Dobrzyn or Dobrin, or Knights of Christ, was a short-lived Polish crusading military order established early in the century to fight the pagan Prussians, and absorbed into the better-known Teutonic Knights in 1235. Its insignia was a red star and sword on a white ground; the sword may sometimes have been doubled – as here, on the surcoat – while the star may sometimes have been in yellow (in heraldic terms, gold). The arms and armour given to the warrior monk in this reconstruction are intended to illustrate a perhaps rather old-fashioned character in what was a relatively backward corner of the Catholic Christian world; for instance, note the one-piece helmet with forward-swept apex. His shield is based upon one of the earliest known represen-tations of a local form that would later become known as the 'Lithuanian pavise'. The emblem of the Order painted on its parchment covering – and partly obscured here – is a more sharply pointed star than the squared form on the surcoat, surmounting a single vertical broadsword, hilt upwards.

The carved effigy of Duke Bolko I of Schweidnitz, c.1301, is in essentially the same style as several military effigies in northern and eastern Germany. Note the large crest on his helm, and the eagle-and-crescent blazon on his shield – compare with Plate C1. Above the duke's right knee a small but unmistakable section of vertical quilting shows that he wears 'soft armour' under his mail hauberk. (*in situ* Cistercian Abbey, Krzerzów)

C3: Eastern Polish infantryman, late 13th century
Based largely upon a little-known but important carved bone or ivory chesspiece found in Cracow (see photos opposite), this foot soldier illustrates the mixture of Western and Eastern traditions which continued to characterize parts of Poland, especially its eastern provinces. His helmet, still of the directly-riveted segmented form, is based upon an example from neighbouring Prussia; here it is attached to the very large mail tippet shown on the chesspiece, rather than

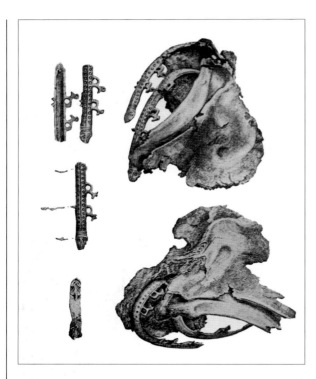

The remains of a leather-covered saddle with decorated bronze mounts, from the cemetery at Lutomiersk near Lodz. (Centre for the Archaeology of Central Poland, Lodz)

to an *aventail*. The cuirass is also based upon the chesspiece, the details of its construction being taken from an inverted lamellar system seen in neighbouring Russia. His sword is of a commonplace European form, but his shield is another early example of the Lithuanian pavise – note the raised vertical 'keel' down the front.

D: FIRST HALF OF THE 14th CENTURY

After a period of fragmentation, the 14th century saw the Kingdom of Poland reunited under a new ruling dynasty, followed by a period of considerable territorial expansion. These processes were accompanied by further 'Westernization' in several aspects of military equipment, architecture and organization; but at the same time Poland was developing its own distinctive styles within the broader Central European tradition.

D1: Mazovian nobleman, mid-14th century

The north-eastern province of Mazovia retained a separate identity and some distinctive military fashions, though these may have been exaggerated in some 14th-century illustrated sources. This figure is based upon a number of images of armoured warriors on Mazovian seals which may themselves have adopted iconography to illustrate links with, or even temporary allegiance to, eastern neighbours such as the Mongol Golden Horde, or the still theoretically pagan Lithuania. The tall, conical, brimmed helmet certainly existed in western Russia, but no examples have yet been found in Poland; here it has also been provided with a mail *aventail*. His armour consists of a short-sleeved mail shirt or *haubergeon* beneath a lamellar cuirass of Eastern inspiration

– such armours certainly spread as far west as the Swedish Baltic island of Gotland north of Poland. The sword is of conventional European type, while the shield is a now-typical Lithuanian pavise. The man's clothes, soft riding boots and saddle also reflect Eastern styles.

D2: Southern Polish knight, early 14th century

In contrast to the Mazovian horseman, this dismounted knight represents the beginnings of a Polish style of relatively light cavalry equipped in regional variations of essentially Western/Central European styles. His helmet is a simple brimmed *chapel-de-fer* worn over a separate mail *coif*. In addition to a mail *hauberk* with separate mittens, he has a simple form of cloth-covered coat-of-plates. His legs are protected by mail *chausses*, quilted *cuisses* (here hidden by the skirt of the coat-of-plates), domed *poleyns* over his knees, plus limited, almost 'bar-shaped' greaves which only cover his shin-bones – these could also be found in parts of Germany. The shield, with a cut-out (still of limited size) at the top right to support a lowered lance, would be further developed in later years, while the more heavily armoured cavalry of Western Europe almost abandoned the use of shields altogether. Its blazon, taken from a contemporary funerary slab, is a symmetrical double-cross-and-arrowhead motif.

D3: Western Polish knight of Buzewoj family, early 14th century

Although the Polish monarchy gradually lost control of most of Silesia during this century, the western aristocracy continued to play a major military role. Their military styles and equipment were now firmly rooted within Central European and particularly German fashions, as typified by this knight's large, heavy 'great helm' and massive crest. His armour is entirely of mail, though worn over and/or beneath thickly padded 'soft armour'. His horse's harness, saddle, bridle and, above all, its heraldic caparison also appear more German than Polish. The family coat-of-arms shown here is repeated on his large 'heater' shield, and note the matching red-and-white sleeve covering the front part of the horse's war-reins.

E: SECOND HALF OF THE 14th CENTURY

Losing some territory in the west, and still being blocked from the Baltic coast by the 'Crusader State' of the Teutonic Knights, Poland again turned southwards and eastwards, becoming dynastically entangled both with Bohemia and Hungary, and starting that process of expansion which would eventually take its forces to the shores of the Black Sea.

E1: Nobleman, late 14th century

By this period the arms and armour of the aristocracy were fully within the wider European tradition. The only significant differences may have been seen in aspects of non-military costume, and in a heraldic language which included motifs that were rare or unknown further west. Most of the armour and weaponry used by this nobleman is likely to have been imported from western Germany, which had become, with Italy, one of the main centres of European arms production. Note the so-called 'dog-faced' bascinet with its mail *aventail*; the plate cuirass, here worn under a fashionably close-tailored surcoat of rich material; and the full plate arm and leg harness. The broad and highly decorated belt of knighthood (obscured here by the saddle) supports a 'ballock' dagger and a relatively short sword, the latter with a retaining chain to a bracket on the breastplate. Once again the horse furniture is indistinguishable from that seen elsewhere in Western/Central Europe, and the heraldic caparison repeats the motif on his shield.

E2: Northern Polish knight in the service of the Lord of Sieradz, mid-14th century
Although at first glance this figure looks essentially the same as his contemporaries in Germany, Scandinavia or Bohemia, much of his armour is probably of local Polish manufacture, if basically in imitation of more expensive German imports. For example, the domed or 'pig-faced' visor on his bascinet is unusual in lacking any ventilation holes other than its single eye-slit. The by now rather archaic cloth-covered coat-of-plates has two anchorage points for retaining chains which, if used, would have run to the hilts of the sword and a dagger. The plate arm-defences are again simple and slightly old-fashioned, as are the *poleyns*, which are the only plate items worn over his mail *chausses*. The distinctively Eastern European style of heraldic design on his shield features a broadsword, hilt low and left, slanting across a bull's mask.

E3: Crossbowman, late 14th century
Although we have illustrated this low-status soldier leading a packhorse here, in fact he would normally be mounted. His equipment is based upon examples excavated from Polish wooden forts that were destroyed by fire in the very late 14th or very early 15th century. The resulting reconstruction looks superficially much the same as comparable troops from Germany or even France, but closer inspection shows several distinctive features. The most obvious is the helmet, made from two pieces of rivetted iron; though essentially a brimmed 'war-hat' its overall shape is unusual, in that there is no angle between the crown and the brim. His old coat-of-plates is made from vertical splints riveted inside a multi-layered cloth exterior, and his only other protection is a short-sleeved mail shirt. His weapons are a normal crossbow with a stave of composite construction; a perhaps mass-produced sword; and an axe, which may be as much a camp-tool as a weapon.

Pack animals were essential to all medieval armies, and huge numbers were required for the long-distance campaigns that were now driving deep into what are today the Ukraine, Moldova and parts of Romania. The pony in this reconstruction is shown as a close relative of the wild Tarpan horse which still roamed much of Eastern Europe; it is perhaps an example of the tough beast also used by the Lithuanians and Teutonic Knights, who called it a *sweik* or *schweike*.

F: FIRST HALF OF THE 15th CENTURY
Although the large Kingdom of Poland and the even larger and fast-expanding Grand Duchy of Lithuania came under the rule of one monarch in 1386, their continuing separate identity was reflected in their military organization and equipment. Poland remained the more urbanized and westward-looking, though much of its flourishing trade was with the east.
F1: Man-at-arms in the service of the Strasy of Odroway and Bialaczow, early 15th century
As long as heavy cavalry continued to dominate Polish (if not

Lithuanian) warfare for most of this century, the heavily armoured men-at-arms continued to rely on imported or locally made full plate 'white harness'. This professional soldier is distinguishable from his Western neighbours solely by the coat-of-arms on his shield and surcoat. This motif, and several other similar examples, had virtually no parallels elsewhere in Europe and were probably rooted in Polish, perhaps Lithuanian, or even Prussian, Russian or Turco-

Effigy of Duke Bolko III of Schweidnitz, made around 1380; compare details – e.g. hat, and chained sword – with Plate E1. (*in situ* Cistercian Abbey, Krzerzów)

Mongol tribal insignia. His armour consists of a large 'dog-faced' bascinet with a rather decorated mail *aventail*; breast and back-plates which are, like the laminated *fauld* around his hips, hidden beneath the close-fitting surcoat; complete plate shoulder and arm harness, to which gauntlets would normally be added in combat; and plate leg harness. Beneath the limb armour his arms and legs are also protected by mail.

F2: Wealthy burgher, mid-15th century
The costume of the wealthy middle class of the cities seems to have retained a number of fashions which proclaimed a distinctive Polish identity. Our reconstructed merchant, inspecting the guard in the timber hoardings which crown his city's walls, wears clothing not of garish colours but of the finest quality woollen materials. The hat has the apperance of two padded rolls of cloth. Two very long tunics are worn layered against the winter cold; the outer one has a standing collar, and amber buttons on the opening down to mid-chest, and both are edged with fine embroidery perhaps including metallic threads. Outer coats with long, very full sleeves might be of rich brocade, lavishly lined with fur, and trimmed not only around the edge and sleeves as here, but sometimes also around the shoulder seams and along the rear sleeve seams; typically they were slit up the back from hem to buttocks, for convenience while riding.

F3: Hand-gunner, mid-15th century
This militiaman is reconstructed from a mixture of surviving or excavated items and pictorial sources. The gunner's unusual helmet survives in a Polish museum, and has been tentatively identified as an earlier bascinet, cut down and remade as a lighter and perhaps cheaper piece. The cloth hood with its scalloped cape is not defensive, but simply a typical outdoor garment of the period, worn here over a dagged-edge mail shirt. Under this is a heavy tunic with simple contrasting edging, slit up the sides from hem to hip; and a pair of woollen hose cut on the bias to give a close fit, with legs of different colours. The curved falchion-like sidearm, with its distinctive hand-guard, is a remarkably early example of the sort of sabre more normally associated with the south-eastern European steppes; however, curved blades had been known earlier in other parts of Europe, and the two traditions might now have been coming together to create the heavier, broader-bladed sabres which became characteristic of both Poland and Hungary. The faceted cast bronze gun, complete with a rampart hook under the barrel, may have been imported from Germany or Hungary, though there is also evidence that such weapons were manufactured in the cities of the Baltic region. The gun's action is still the simplest form of matchlock, initiated with a smouldering slowmatch thrust into a shallow priming pan above a touchhole in the upper surface of the breech. The box on the floor holds balls and measured, wrapped or bagged powder charges (for which there is Western European evidence from at least the 1470s), and the horn contains loose gunpowder.

G: SECOND HALF OF THE 15th CENTURY
The vast combined state of Poland-Lithuania was not the only imperial power to be struggling for domination north-west of the Black Sea; here Polish armies were in competition with Hungary and the rapidly expanding Ottoman Turkish sultanate, with local states such as Moldova caught in the middle. Further east the Lithuanians – if not yet usually the Poles – also clashed with the fragmented remnants of the Mongol Horde, of which the most powerful was the Khanate of the Crimea.

G1: Man-at-arms, mid- to late 15th century
After about 1450 there was an increasingly clear distinction between the heavy cavalry men-at-arms who had dominated Polish armies for centuries, and the light cavalry who were becoming increasingly important in the sort of far-ranging and fluid campaigns that Polish forces were now undertaking. This reconstruction is based upon Polish illustrated sources, including funerary monuments, which portray some interesting variations on European 'white harness' of this period. Under his conventional visored sallet, with a feather plume, his shoulder-length hair would be folded up on top of his head inside the helmet padding. He wears no *bevor* to protect throat and chin, relying on the padded standing collar of his mail tippet. The shoulder-protecting *pauldrons* are rather simplified, and he has only one unusually large *rondel* protecting the front of his right shoulder; this strongly suggests that he would still carry a shield into combat. There are some unusually shaped additional plates above and below the elbow and knee joints; this might also suggest that the quality of steel used in this perhaps locally manufactured armour was inferior to that of the best imported armours, and so needed reinforcement.

G2: Eastern Polish light cavalryman, late 15th century
As yet even the light cavalry still seem to have worn armour, although within a generation or so Polish light horse were apparently entirely unarmoured. This reflected changes in weaponry as well as tactics, and consequently this figure has been interpreted as what might better be described as a 'lighter' rather than strictly a 'light' cavalryman. His legs are now unprotected but he still has a long-sleeved mail *hauberk* and a substantial broad-brimmed 'war-hat' of globose shape, forged from a single piece of metal. The fact that he has a breast-plate and some plate arm protection might perhaps identify him as an officer of light horse, whose men would simply have worn the mail shirt and a helmet. His horse's harness has yet to change much, though the saddle is clearly rooted in the riding traditions of Eastern Europe rather than that of the 'knightly' cavalry of the West. The harness has decorative rosettes, and note the bell behind the saddle; the broad war-reins – obscured here – would also have rosettes and pendent bells.

G3: Mercenary crossbowman, late 15th century
In complete contrast, Polish infantry continued to include professional or mercenary troops whose armour was as complete – and presumably as heavy – as that of the heavy cavalry. Though based upon Polish pictorial sources, and incorporating some elements of decoration that seem to have been popular in Eastern/Central Europe, the basic armour is virtually identical to that used in Germany, Bohemia and some parts of Hungary. The helmet is a visored sallet; typically the visor might have an inner border of gilded decoration. It would be worn with a plate *bevor* to protect the throat. There are massive but simple one-piece *pauldrons* over the shoulders; the body defences are breast and back-plates with a *plackart*, and a laminated *fauld* around the hips. He wears complete plate arm and leg harness; the outer plate on the forearms (*rerebraces*) and upper arms (*vambraces*) are fluted in chevron patterns, for

The magnificent effigial slab of Piotr Salomon, dating from around 1516 – see Plate H1. Note the tall hat with a folded brim, the shoulder-length hair, the rich brocade coat worn over his armour, the two-handed sword, and the swan blazon on the shield at his feet. (*in situ* Church of St Mary, Cracow)

additional strength. The soldier's role as an infantry crossbowman is, however, indicated by his lack of *sabatons* or armoured shoes, and his gauntlets would lack scales covering the lower part of the fingers. He is propping up the pavise which will shelter him while he reloads his substantial composite-stave crossbow with its windlass. For close work he has a war-axe.

H: EARLY 16th CENTURY

In this period Poland-Lithuania faced the rising power of the Russian state of Muscovy. Most clashes involved Lithuanian rather than Polish forces, but both were sometimes caught up in what would later become one of the most widespread struggles of early modern European history.

H1: Army commander, early 16th century

Records indicate that it was normal for senior commanders not to wear helmets in battle; they needed to be immediately recognizable, and were not expected to take a personal part in the fighting. In this reconstruction we give the commander

the tall hat and magnificent fur-trimmed coat which are shown in the effigial slab of Piotr Salomon in the Church of St Mary, Cracow (see photo, left). His armour is either in Italian style or of Italian manufacture; its laminated steel *sabatons* have the broad, rounded toes that were now coming into fashion to replace the elongated, pointed toes of the previous century. Little is known about Polish horse-armour at this period; while the commander's armour is essentially Italian, that of his horse is interpreted as German and reconstructed as a simplified version of one illustrated in the 'Triumph of the Emperor Maximilian' engravings – which include pictures of both Central and Eastern European troops.

H2: Hussar, c.1520

The battle of Orsha, in which a Polish-Lithuanian army defeated a Muscovite force in 1514, was not the most important clash of the period, but it was the subject of a large and detailed painting made only a few years after the event; this light cavalryman is based on hussars who feature prominently in this painting (see photo, page 38). He is an early representative of a new style of light cavalry that would eventually play a major role in almost all European armies. The quilted cap worn beneath his remarkable 'top hat' may have included some protective metal element, if only of mail. Otherwise the rider has no armour whatsoever, and could protect himself only with a shield (this is not illustrated here, but was almost rectangular, with an upswept pointed extension of the top left corner and a small cut-out in the top right corner). Note the coat with its flamboyant braiding and frogging, and the slit thighs of the hose, showing a contrasting colour beneath. The soft boots are slit right down the outside and fastened by pairs of brass buttons and laces; note the gilded, tooled leather flap or 'Mercury's wing' attached to the boot instep – this was removed when not in the saddle. His sidearms are a broad sabre, suspended in Eastern style from under a sash; and a flanged iron mace, with a wooden shaft and bronze grip, thrust into it. The horse has a shaped blanket or partial caparison over its rump, fringed, brightly decorated, and bearing a plume from a brass boss. The saddlery and harness are thoroughly Eastern; note the decorative throat-lash.

H3: Man-at-arms armoured for foot combat, early 16th century

If the Polish hussar represented the future of European cavalry warfare, this remarkably heavily armoured foot soldier represents the end of a long tradition of European infantry fighting. His sallet helmet, with its visor beaten into the shape of a 'nose', was probably a Polish style, and perhaps a localized one. He wears the best quality of Western armour, with a massive *bevor* and *pauldrons* and complete arm and leg harness; the breast-plate even has three holes where a lance-rest could be bolted on, emphasizing that this armour could have been used on horseback as well as on foot. The broad, laminated steel skirt is, however, only for use on foot, and replaces the shallower *fauld* used on horseback. Such steel skirts were more commonly used in tournaments than in real battle, but they are shown on the front rank of fully armoured Polish foot soldiers in the painting of the battle of Orsha. He is armed with a partizan polearm and a two-handed sword; the large keeled pavise, propped up with a pole, is painted with an image of St George.

INDEX

Figures in **bold** refer to illustrations.